Nixonomics

Nixonomics

SECOND EDITION

Leonard Silk

PRAEGER PUBLISHERS
New York • Washington • London

Material in NIXONOMICS appeared as "Wanted: A More Human, Less Dismal Science," in *Saturday Review,* January 22, 1972, © 1972 Saturday Review, Inc.

PRAEGER PUBLISHERS
111 Fourth Avenue, New York, N.Y. 10003, U.S.A.
5, Cromwell Place, London SW7 2JL, England

Published in the United States of America in 1973
by Praeger Publishers, Inc.

This is the second edition of a book originally published by
Praeger Publishers, Inc., in 1972.

Library of Congress Catalog Card Number: 72-185654

Printed in the United States of America

Contents

To the Memory of My Father

HARRY L. SILK

Newsboy Businessman Political Reformer

Acknowledgments

Adam, Andrew, Bernice, and Mark Silk have read parts of the manuscript of this book and have given me their advice and sympathy, which I appreciate greatly. But I am solely responsible for the faults of the book.

I am grateful to Mrs. Miriam Klipper for her sensitive and thoughtful editing, and to Miss Linda Martin and Miss Mary Lou Shaffer for valuable research assistance.

I owe my thanks to the editors of *The New York Times, Daedalus, The Saturday Review,* the *American Economic Review,* and the Duke University Press for permission to draw upon previously published articles of mine; much of this earlier material, however, has been altered, rewritten, or expanded upon.

LEONARD SILK

Montclair, New Jersey

Prologue

Oh! for a Muse of reportage that could ascend
The brightest heavens in a ship of space
Electronically to inspect the land below,
The White House penetrate, economists overhear.
And soft-voiced courtiers catch upon a tape.
Then should the cunning Richard, like himself,
Enter the Oval Chamber; and at his heels,
Leash'd in like hounds, should Connally, Shultz, and Stein
Crouch for employment. But pardon, gentles all,
The flat pedestrian spirit that hath dared
From drafty Tenth Floor office off Times Square
On these unworthy pages to set forth
So great an object; can this volume hold
The grossest national product of our land,

And disclose the policy-making of our chiefs?
Can we cram within these boards the very thoughts
That did affright the working class when prices soared,
And jobs were rubbed away like blackboard chalk?
Dare we hearken back to bad old days,
When counselors cried, "Oh, pardon! A crooked figure
May attest in little place a billion;
Let us cipher to this great account
On your imagination. We meant well!"
Then within the compass of this tome
You'd see the angry Richard, red as on a color screen;
He calleth for a change in Game Plan One,
Bestows controls on wages, prices, rents,
Lest dogs of inflation slip their leads
And run through the streets baying,
"Nay! Vote not for Richard! He's for laissez-faire!"
Ah, that was a plan that went sickly sour.
Its authors have been purged, save for Shultz and Stein.
The others are no more. The ghost of Friedman
Haunts his Gothic walls. Peace hath Richard made
With Arthur Burns; the stock of money bubbles,
The jobless rate to melt. Deep in deficit
Our hero lies, completely unashamed. Goldwaterites
Gnash their teeth in Phoenix and L.A.,
But Richard hath a rendezvous to keep
As usual on election day.
Your thoughts I need to clothe my themes,
Turning the deeds and dreads of sev'ral years
Into an hour-glass; for the which supply
Admit me Chorus to this history;
Who prologue-like beg your humble patience not to fail,
While I unfold my version of this economic tale.

1. Voices in the Air

Inflation was the major economic problem that Richard Nixon inherited from Lyndon B. Johnson. "There is some kind of malevolent law about the rhythm of political life that puts some of us here when it is hard to be a hero," said Paul W. McCracken, Mr. Nixon's first chairman of the Council of Economic Advisers, a few days before the inauguration.

While Mr. Nixon fully understood the necessity of putting the economy through what he called "slowing pains," he was determined to avoid a full-scale recession and sharp increase in unemployment—say, to the 7 per cent level, which it attained during the 1960–61 recession. That slump had cost Mr. Nixon the White House in his campaign against John F. Kennedy. Mr. Nixon's economists assured him that they thought it would be possible to check the inflation without causing a real recession; at his very first press conference after taking office in 1969, Mr. Nixon declared, "I want to emphasize that we believe it is possible to control inflation without increasing unemployment in, certainly, any substantial way."

To accomplish this objective, the Administration adopted what came to be called the policy of "gradualism"; it apparently got its name from the statement of Chairman McCracken on January 28, 1969, that the job of stopping inflation "will have to be done easily. It will have to be done gradually."

The major weapon that the Nixon Administration counted on to achieve a gradual victory over inflation was a "Friedmanesque" monetary policy. Mr. Nixon's economists had been much influenced by the theory of Professor Milton Friedman of the University of Chicago that changes in the supply of money resulting from the actions of the Federal Reserve System caused changes in total spending by businesses and consumers—and hence changes in both the real output of goods and services and in the over-all level of prices.

If the Federal Reserve increased the money supply faster than the American economy was capable of increasing the output of real goods and services, prices would rise. But if the Federal Reserve held the growth of the money supply well below the economy's potential output, prices would weaken, real output would decline, and unemployment would rise. And if the money supply were to be forced or permitted to shrink over a long enough period of time, deep depression, deflation, and mass unemployment would result—as happened in the 1930's.

To avoid the extremes of inflation and depression, Professor Friedman proposed a simple rule: Require the Federal Reserve to keep the money supply growing at the same rate as the potential growth in output of real goods and services.

Dr. Friedman, whose great gift as a teacher is that he puts matters simply and unequivocally, laid down a hard rule for the Federal Reserve: "I would specify that the Reserve System shall see to it that the total stock of money . . . rises month by month, and indeed, so far as possible, day by day, at an annual rate of X percent, where X is some number between 3 and 5."

The reason why Professor Friedman chose a money-supply growth rate between those two numbers is that the long-term growth rate of real goods and services in the United States lies between 3 and 5 per cent per annum.

The economists who came to Washington with Mr. Nixon did not intend to follow the Friedman rule slavishly; indeed, they could not if they had wanted to, since the Federal Reserve Board has independent or quasi-independent status. Also, there were technical complications; for instance, it was far from clear how one should define the stock of money. Professor Henry Wallich of Yale University, who served as a member of the Council of Economic Advisers under President Dwight D. Eisenhower, and who became chief economic consultant to the Secretary of the Treasury in the Nixon Administration, has counted ten different definitions of the money supply. Professor Friedman himself had sometimes preferred to use the definition he calls M_1—currency outside commercial banks, plus all demand deposits of commercial banks—and has sometimes used M_2—currency in circulation, plus demand deposits, plus time and savings deposits. But Professor Friedman regarded such complications as no serious deterrent to the use of his rule: "The precise definition of money adopted, or the precise rate of growth chosen makes far less difference than the definite choice of a particular definition and a particular rate of growth."

There are, in fact, great complexities in determining how to calculate the rate of growth in the money supply under whatever definition. Should this be done from one month to the next, and then annualized? Or from year to year? Or perhaps from day to day, as Dr. Friedman himself suggested as ideal? Federal Reserve officials insist that they do not have the ability to bring about such a result, even if this were assumed to be a desirable objective. The Federal Reserve Open Market Committee seeks to determine what the supply of money will be—and what the level of interest rates and credit conditions will be—by regulating the ability of commercial banks to make loans; but there is considerable variation in the degree and time lag of both the banks and the borrowing and spending public in responding to changes in Federal Reserve policy. These variations depend partly on states of confidence and expectations of future business conditions and the opportunity for profit. As the eminent British economist Sir John Hicks has put it:

> Money is not a mechanism: it is a human institution, one of the most remarkable of human institutions. Even the simplest forms of money, even metallic coinage, even the use of metals as money that preceded coinage, none can function without some minimum of trust. . . . A fully developed monetary system (as so far experienced) is very sensitive, and is therefore unstable.

Mr. Nixon's economists were by no means unaware of these complexities surrounding an application of Friedman's money-supply rule; they were, after all, "Friedmanesque," as Paul McCracken described himself, rather than "Friedmanite." Yet Professor Friedman's rule, if pragmatically applied, had overwhelming appeal to an Administration that did not want to increase taxes as a means of stopping inflation. The Nixon economists considered fiscal policy (favored by the New Economists of the Kennedy and Johnson administrations) to have failed because of the political difficulty of making prompt and appropriate adjustments ("fine tuning") in tax rates or in government expenditures. Possessed of a conservative ideology, they sought to reduce or at least restrain the growth of federal government spending; higher taxes, even if needed as a means of promoting economic stability, were regarded by the Nixonians as likely to result in higher government expenditures. And they apparently believed—as Friedman certainly did—that the way to cut government spending was to cut taxes, not vice versa.

Friedman's money-supply rule was also appealing in that it did not require the Nixon Administration to intervene, as both the Kennedy and Johnson administrations had, in the wage-and-price decisions of labor and business. The Friedman theory asserted that such government interference, insofar as it was able actually to influence or control certain wage rates and prices, would only distort the use of resources, unfairly hurt particular companies or workers, and have no effect at all on the general level of prices, this being a function of the growth of the money supply in relation to the capacity of the economic system to produce real goods and services. Mr. Nixon himself took an extremely hostile line against wage-and-price guideposts; he equated them with direct wage-and-price controls, which he said he had come to loathe as a young lawyer in the Office of Price Administration during World War II.

Mr. Nixon's Secretary of Labor George P. Shultz, later to become director of the Office of Management and Budget

and for a while the President's most important economic
adviser, had a long-standing skepticism and antipathy toward
guideposts, both as an economist-neighbor of Professor
Friedman's at the University of Chicago and as an experienced labor arbitrator. Most importantly, however, Mr.
Nixon and his aides considered that the guideposts were
dead when they took office—destroyed by the rampant de-
mand-pull inflation that they had inherited from President
Johnson. The job of checking inflation would have to be
done by getting rid of excess demand; jawboning or guideposts would be a waste of energy, a political liability, and,
since the results would doubtless be negligible, a blow to
presidential prestige. Organized labor had not put Mr.
Nixon in the White House and was most unlikely to respond
to his pleas for wage restraint; it seemed unfair and unwise
to put the entire burden of price restraint on big and con-
spicuous businesses, which might feel bound to be more
responsive to presidential appeals or censure.

Soon after becoming President, Mr. Nixon publicly affirmed his decision not to exhort labor leaders or businessmen to restrain their wage or price decisions, because "much
as these men might personally want to do what is in the best
interest of the nation, they have to be guided by the interests of the organizations that they represent." One business advisory service promptly translated the presidential
message into simpler language for its clients: "The President
has just said you can raise prices."

The fundamental economic policies that the Nixon Administration held when it assumed office, then, were a Friedmanesque monetary policy, a fiscal policy aimed more at
checking the growth of federal expenditures than at economic stabilization, and a laissez-faire policy toward price-
and-wage decisions by industry and labor.

The Chairman of the Federal Reserve Board at the start of the Nixon Administration was the veteran William McChesney Martin, who had long practiced the art of seeking to adapt Federal Reserve policies to those of the Administration in office—without compromising his own principles, among which staunch opposition to inflation was perhaps number one. However, Mr. Martin had often stressed that the Federal Reserve also pursued the objectives of "maximum employment, production, and purchasing power" specified by the Employment Act of 1946.

Mr. Martin and his staff were not enamored of their archcritic, Professor Friedman; nevertheless, the record suggests that the Federal Reserve sought to pursue policies in the first half of 1969 consistent with the steady monetary-growth rule favored by the Nixon Administration's economists, including Arthur F. Burns, who was in the White House as counselor to the President. Dr. Burns had been chairman of the Council of Economic Advisers under President Eisenhower and had been an old and trusted adviser of Mr. Nixon's since his days as Vice President.

To be sure, it appeared during the first half of 1969 that the money supply was growing at an annual rate of only about 2 to 3 per cent; Professor Friedman sharply criticized the Federal Reserve for being too restrictive and threatening to put the economy into a recession. However, the preliminary data on which Professor Friedman based his attack proved to be faulty. When they were later revised, it turned out that, from December, 1968, to June, 1969, the money supply—defined as demand deposits plus currency in circulation, the M_1 concept—increased by 4.4 per cent. This was just the rate of growth the doctor from Chicago had prescribed.

During the first half of 1969, the consumer price index

rose at an annual rate of 5.8 per cent, somewhat faster than consumer prices had risen during the last twelve months of the Johnson Administration, when they had climbed 4.6 per cent. However, monetary policy was supposed to operate with a lag, which Professor Friedman thought would be about six months. Thus, the price performance of the first six months of the Nixon Administration could be blamed on the excessively rapid rate of growth of the money supply during the preceding six months of the Johnson Administration; from June, 1968, to December, 1968, the money supply had increased at an annual rate of 7.1 per cent—and the money supply plus time deposits had risen at an annual rate of 12.5 per cent.

But, in the second half of 1969, the price performance was no better than it had been in the first half, despite slower monetary growth; the consumer price index rose at an annual rate of 5.8 per cent from June, 1969, to December, 1969. The lag of price change behind money-supply change was clearly turning out to be longer than the six-month period that Professor Friedman had anticipated. In August, 1969, Dr. Friedman wrote: "If the rate of price rise has not begun to abate by the fourth quarter of this year, it will be time to ask us for an explanation." The inflation did not abate; and the only explanation was that the time lags were apparently longer and more indeterminate than earlier assumed.

But Chairman Martin and his colleagues at the Federal Reserve Board, alarmed about the continuing course of the inflation, decided that they had been too lax. From June, 1969, to December, 1969, the money supply was held to an annual rate of growth of 0.6 per cent—virtually no growth at all. Industrial production began to decline in July. Gross national product (GNP), deflated for price change, declined slightly in the fourth quarter of 1969 and began to drop at

an annual rate of 3 per cent in the first quarter of 1970.
President Nixon sent Arthur F. Burns to replace William
McChesney Martin as chairman of the Federal Reserve
Board. The monetarists blamed Martin as the cause of all
the trouble. But, despite the slump, inflation still did not
slacken, as measured by the consumer price index. During
the first six months of 1970, following the preceding 0.6 per
cent growth rate of the money supply, *consumer prices rose
at an annual rate of 6 per cent*. Real output had taken the
whole impact of the slowdown in monetary growth; unemployment, which had averaged 3.5 per cent in 1969, climbed
to 5 per cent in May, 1970.

Business confidence suffered a rude blow. The economy
was slipping into a recession, with no tangible evidence that
inflation was abating. Interest rates had climbed to levels not
seen in a hundred years, with devastating effects on housing.
The federal budget was dropping into deficit, aggravating
pressures on money markets. The stock market went into
the worst decline it had experienced since the Great Depression.

International developments worsened the problem. It was
the worry that the Cambodian invasion by U.S. troops would
cause a massive increase in government spending, and hence
in the federal debt and pressure on the money market, that
put Wall Street into such a fright during May. Suddenly the
specter of another 1929 became starkly real. Mr. Nixon
sought to rally the market by declaring that if he had any
money, he would be buying stocks himself. He assured the
nation that he meant to pull U.S. troops out of Cambodia
by June and continue to withdraw them from Vietnam. The
President's reassurances that he meant to "wind down" and
"Vietnamize" the war appear to have been the chief factor
in bracing investor confidence.

But there was another serious problem worrying business

—that of a liquidity squeeze, which seemed to be threatening some businesses with financial disaster, a threat made all too credible by the collapse in June, 1970, of the mammoth Penn Central Railroad, the greatest business failure in history.

The Federal Reserve's tight money policies during the latter part of 1969 were clearly involved in the liquidity squeeze. Chairman Burns of the Federal Reserve Board, facing a potential monetary panic, now threw Friedmanism to the winds and began to pour money into the economy. During the year following the near-panic of May, 1970, M_1 grew by 8.5 per cent and M_2 by 13 per cent, rates double or triple the Friedman prescription.

Arthur Burns is famous as a pragmatist. During the Eisenhower Administration, his policy prescriptions were essentially Keynesian, though he had been known earlier as a sharp critic of Keynesian doctrines. Burns's pragmatism had long made him a critic of the doctrinaire Friedman, his longtime associate at the National Bureau of Economic Research, where Friedman was very much junior to Burns, the inheritor of Wesley C. Mitchell's mantle. Burns's eclecticism had permitted him to assimilate that portion of Friedmanian monetary policy that he regarded as valid and appropriate to the political and economic needs of the time—or to cast it aside when circumstances demanded it.

At President Nixon's blue-ribbon dinner for forty-two businessmen and stock brokers at the White House on May 27, 1970, when Mr. Nixon was striving to rebuild business confidence, Dr. Burns declared that no rigid rule on how rapidly the money supply should be allowed to grow would deter the Federal Reserve from supplying more money in case of a liquidity crisis. The Federal Reserve, he said, would discharge its responsibilities as a "lender of last resort," and businessmen had no need to worry about the Federal's alertness or its ability to supply the money needs of the country. The Federal Reserve, Dr. Burns declared, "would not let the economy collapse."

Dr. Burns, a man of strong will, had already brought this point of view to bear on the other members of the Federal Reserve Board and the Open Market Committee. With the stock market and business in a state of acute jitters, the Open Market Committee, on May 26, 1970, decided to concentrate for a while on keeping financial conditions calm rather than achieving a "target" growth of the money supply—as the record of the meeting showed when published three months later. "The members agreed," the minutes read,

> that moderate growth in money and bank credit remained the appropriate longer-run objective of policy. They concluded, however, that it was necessary at present to give priority to the objective of moderating pressures on financial markets, recognizing that that might temporarily entail higher growth rates in the monetary aggregates than were considered appropriate for the longer run.

But the damage was done, and the President's hopes of avoiding a recession had been shattered. There was a marked slowdown in real economic output and a rise in unemployment from 2.7 million workers out of jobs at the end of 1969 to more than 5 million by the end of 1970. The slump and the continuing inflation resulted in a political setback for the Republican Party in the congressional and gubernatorial elections of November, 1970.

With inflation continuing despite the climb in unemployment, Burns also demonstrated his pragmatism by becoming one of the first of Mr. Nixon's advisers [1] to come out for

---

[1] Two other "premature" supporters of an incomes policy were Assistant Secretary of the Treasury Murray L. Weidenbaum and Assistant Budget Director Maurice Mann, the "2 M's." Both had left the Administration well before August 15, 1971.

an "incomes policy"—that is, a program to restrain inflationary wage-and-price decisions of business and labor by presidential persuasion and pressure. As in his attitude toward Keynesian economic policies, Dr. Burns had formerly been a sharp critic of wage-price guideposts.[2] But he decided as 1970 wore on that it was essential to face up to the fact that, while tight money had brought the economy's expansion to a halt and had caused unemployment to rise, it had not stopped inflation. Although the members of the Council of Economic Advisers continued to insist that their "game plan" was going just about on schedule, one high Administration official bitterly remarked (in private), "Sure, we're on schedule—we're ahead of schedule in getting to high unemployment and we're behind schedule in reducing excessive inflation. Just average those two things out, and you can see we're on schedule." Nevertheless, the Friedmanians in the Administration continued to regard wage-price curbs as tools of the devil.

But, since politics provides tests as severe as those of the marketplace, Friedmanism suffered a setback—though not a complete sellout—within the Nixon Administration. After the November, 1970, election, Mr. Nixon made the startling remark, "I am now a Keynesian." This apparently meant that he was no longer a budget-balancer. He and his economic advisers said they believed in the concept of a "full-employment budget"—one in which revenues would equal expenditures only if the economy were at full employment. But Mr. Nixon's advisers—especially the Chicagoan monetarists George Shultz and Herbert Stein—resisted the Keynesian label, which was anathema to good Friedmanians. Stein, who had provided an early post–World War II

[2] See his Fairless Lectures, *The Management of Prosperity* (Pittsburgh: Carnegie Institute of Technology, 1965).

formulation of the full-employment budget concept for the Committee for Economic Development, a private research and policy group sponsored by the heads of large business organizations, publicized the conservative Republican roots of the full-employment surplus. Friedman also reminded the world that he had thought up the full-employment surplus rule.

However, the President's economists sought to persuade the Federal Reserve Board to increase the rate of growth of the money supply much faster than the Friedman formula of 3 to 5 per cent growth would have allowed. The President's economists apparently wanted monetary growth in excess of 8 per cent—and perhaps as high as 12 per cent—to speed up the economy. And they got what they asked for.

Outside the Administration, the assault on Friedmanism was furious. Professor Paul Samuelson of M.I.T. said that Friedman had come forth as "an alleged challenger to the mantle of Keynes," but that "his notions that only rates of change in the money supply can be expected to have predictable effects on the aggregate of money Gross National Product have not been found convincing by most economists." Professor Samuelson said that when he was asked, "Is Keynes dead?," his answer was, "Yes. And so are Newton and Einstein."

Perhaps Professor Samuelson's views might be dismissed as biased—by his past commitment to Keynesianism and by his political affiliations with the Democratic Party. Nevertheless, it soon became evident that disarray had broken out among the monetarists and some influential sympathizers were shifting against Friedmanism. For instance, Professor Harry G. Johnson, a colleague of Professor Friedman's at the University of Chicago who was regarded as close to the monetarists, delivered a slashing attack on Friedmanism at the annual meeting of the American Economic Association in December, 1970. Professor Johnson said that the monetarist doctrine was analytically weak and predicted that Professor Friedman's attempted counterrevolution to Keynes would peter out and, indeed, had already begun to do so.

Professor Johnson said that, by the 1960's, the Keynesian revolution had been ripe for a counterattack, because it had failed to solve the problem of inflation. He contended that the monetarist effort at a counterrevolution was also sparked by the same social force that had touched off the Keynesian revolution—the burning passion of young economists to overthrow their profession's aging Establishment. At last, with the election of Richard Nixon to the Presidency, the monetarists had their chance—and failed.

On August 15, 1971, the two-and-a-half-year experiment in economic gradualism and laissez faire came to an abrupt end. Mr. Nixon froze wages, prices, and rents and called for tax cuts, especially for business, to stimulate the economy. The former Democratic Governor of Texas, Secretary of the Treasury John B. Connally, began talking down interest rates in the "give-'em-hell" style of L.B.J. Mr. Nixon's old mentor, Chairman Arthur Burns of the Federal Reserve Board—who had been in the doghouse just a couple of weeks earlier for pressing the White House to adopt an incomes policy—had won his long campaign for wage-and-price restraints.

And, at the University of Chicago, Professor Friedman, whose ideas more than any other's had shaped the earlier Nixonian gradualist policy, expressed his deep unhappiness over the switch; he expected the controls to be ineffective, and he denounced them as fundamentally immoral, because they interfered with economic freedom. Professor

Friedman's former colleague at Chicago and his warmest champion in the White House, George P. Shultz, who had scored a signal victory in defense of what he called the "steady-as-you-go" policy at a Camp David weekend at the end of June, had seen the boldly activist Secretary Connally emerge victorious from the second Camp David weekend in mid-August.

What caused the dramatic switch?

In mid-August, 1971, the election of 1972 was only a bit more than fourteen months away. But public-opinion experts, including such experienced politicians as Mr. Nixon, know that you cannot turn public opinion around on a dime on so fundamental an issue as the state of the economy on the eve of an election; the President had only about nine to twelve months at most if he were to stand for re-election on a peace-and-prosperity platform. In mid-summer of 1971, unemployment was still hanging around 6 per cent of the labor force. Inflation was still above a 4 per cent rate. It had become clear, said Paul McCracken, "that working the rate of inflation lower, in the absence of further measures, would be hard going—and certainly without more vigorous measures of expansion." Costs of production were still rising steadily; the industrial wholesale price index, climbing at a 4.5 per cent rate, was not, as McCracken said, "providing the basis for further stability of consumer prices." And, as an immediate trigger, the nation's balance of payments was going to pot; the dollar was under heavy attack. Hot money was rushing out of the country. In the third quarter of 1971, the U.S. balance of payments, on an official settlements basis, plunged to an incredibly high annual rate of deficit—$48 billion.

So Mr. Nixon finally moved. The President's monetarist counselors could say, "Ah, if only he had waited a little longer," or, "Politics set the limit on what sound economic doctrine could achieve," but Mr. Nixon was unwilling to sink with a policy for which he obviously had warm ideological sympathy. It would be no minor criticism of the monetarist economic doctrine to say that nothing was wrong with it but the political constraints. However, the doctrine also failed economically, in its own terms. Inflation did *not* fade away.

What appears to have been fundamentally responsible for the failure of the Friedmanesque "new, new economics" was that it assumed that the American economy bore a close resemblance to Adam Smith's image of a highly competitive system. Mr. Nixon's advisers believed, with Smith, that government could intervene in the private economy only foolishly or disastrously. Inflation, they held, could be caused only by too much money, not by business or labor power.

But the American economy has drifted farther and farther from the Smithian competitive model, as private monopolies in product and labor markets have grown. After President Nixon launched his New Economic Policy (N.E.P.) on August 15, 1971, Secretary of the Treasury John B. Connally was asked whether the "American economy is out of kilter because big unions and big corporations have acquired the power to impose wage-price packages on the rest of the economy." Mr. Connally answered, "I think there is much to be said for that. Yes, I think at some point in the not-too-distant future we're going to have to take a look at the capacity of big business and big labor to abuse power in this country."

The American society is held together by a system of rights and duties and restraints—or, as Walter Lippmann once put it, "by a slightly antiquated formulation of the balance of power among the active interests in the community." When powerful groups cannot work out an adjustment of their conflicts without hurting the rest of the community, public opinion is brought to bear—and public officials must intervene to effect a better balance among community interests.

That is the point at which the conservative Administration of Richard Nixon had arrived in the late summer of 1971.

2. Mr. Nixon's Conservatism

Democratic presidents customarily attach labels to their political and economic philosophies. Thus, there were Woodrow Wilson's New Freedom, Franklin D. Roosevelt's New Deal, Harry Truman's Fair Deal, John F. Kennedy's New Frontier, and Lyndon B. Johnson's Great Society. Republican presidents are much less given to such brand labeling. True, Theodore Roosevelt, a maverick among Republicans, named his philosophy the New Nationalism. This was the doctrine that he opposed to the New Freedom of Woodrow Wilson, with its stress on the virtue of competition and the curse of bigness.

Instead, Teddy Roosevelt held that concentration of economic power was the inevitable result of mass production and technological advance. He thought it was better to worry less about preserving competition than about developing national controls to ensure that the benefits of modern industrialism were more evenly distributed. Teddy Roosevelt's views now seem closer to those of Professor John Kenneth Galbraith than to those of Presidents Warren G. Harding, Calvin Coolidge, Herbert Hoover, or Dwight D. Eisenhower.

Since the first Roosevelt's New Nationalism, other Republican chiefs of state have let their ideologies go unchristened. Reversion to a more modest and passive role for government—the normal stance of Republican presidents—scarcely lends itself to highfalutin titles. Harding's "Back to Normalcy" was a useful campaign slogan, and Coolidge's "The Business of America Is Business" pleased the business community, but historians use both slogans ironically as the self-indictments of short-sighted leaders.

President Nixon has not tried to attach a formal title to his Administration. In line with his initial objective of cooling the rhetoric after President Johnson's Great Society, a fancy new label apparently seemed inappropriate to him. Yet the Nixon Administration deserves a title, since it has evolved a philosophy that plays a crucial role in determining the President's approach to the national budget, taxation, military policy, national priorities, monetary policy, foreign trade, wages and prices, race relations, welfare, government-business relations, and much else.

Before a name can be given to the Nixon philosophy, however, it must be more clearly defined. Obviously, it is conservative. But that doesn't say much, since there are many varieties of conservatism.

During the Goldwater campaign of 1964, Herbert Stein, later to become the second chairman of President Nixon's Council of Economic Advisers, pointed out three distinct varieties of conservative economics, which he labeled New York Conservatism, Chicago Conservatism, and Main Street Conservatism.

New York Conservatism, Mr. Stein pointed out, might once have been called Wall Street thinking, but he suggested that Park Avenue thinking might be more appropriate with the changing location of high corporate offices in New York City. The New York brand of conservatism is not, however, simply a rationalization of the private interests of big business. It seeks to identify business interests with those of the broad society—and so it favors modern fiscal policy to promote full employment, liberal trade policies to tie the free world together, international defense treaties and foreign aid to stem the tide of Communism, and a rather close partnership between business and government. Indeed, the New York view is that business should accept the fact that it has certain important social responsibilities to fulfill. Its intellectual stronghold is the Committee for Economic Development.

The New York creed radiates to other localities—but its popularity diminishes as it spreads westward. It has been ferociously attacked—for instance, by Senator Barry Goldwater—as the ideology of the Eastern Establishment. President Nixon has ties to Wall Street and Park Avenue, but he had even stronger political links to the anti-Eastern Establishment. His own heartland, after all, is in Southern California.

Chicago Conservatism takes its name from the Department of Economics of the University of Chicago. Its grand mogul, of course, is Professor Milton Friedman. Professor Friedman, as we have seen, had a major impact on Nixonian monetary policy and also on such diverse matters as the Family Assistance Plan, the voluntary draft, and the President's initial opposition to wage-and-price guideposts. The Administration has adopted policies far removed from those of Chicagoism, but its laissez-faire philosophy appears to remain the center of Mr. Nixon's heart's desire.

Main Street Conservatism is the conservatism of the rural or small-town Congressman, businessman, editor, lawyer, doctor, and clergyman. It has no formal ideology, but Herbert Stein suggests it is probably the most influential of the three brands of conservatism. Its hero is the little man—the independent retailer, the real estate dealer, the builder, the family farmer, the general practitioner. He does not particularly like competition nor want it. "His virtue," said Mr. Stein,

> does not have to be found in what he contributes to the Society. His virtue is in what he is, in his independence and in the moral qualities associated with it. A good Society is one in which there are many like him, and it is the function of the Society, paradoxical as it may sound, to protect his existence and independence.

He likes—and gets—fair trade laws. He likes—and gets—farm subsidies, cheap credit, and many other government benefactions. He likes protection from foreign competition—and he is in the midst of a big drive now to get more of it. He has many friends in the Administration, and even more in Congress. Indeed, Mr. Nixon reveres his qualities. He is the Middle American.

But Mr. Stein's three brands of conservatism do not exhaust the list. There is also what I would call Texas Conservatism (oil), South Carolina Conservatism (textiles and opposition to racial desegregation), Peter Drucker Conservatism (big government is sick and weak; smaller but stronger government is needed), and Moral Conservatism (up with people with white hats, like John Wayne and

Billy Graham; down with people with black hats, like Phillip Roth and Elaine May).

Mr. Nixon finds happiness in all the various conservative creeds and strives to mediate among them. And there we find the right name for his Administration—the Happy Medium! There we find the true Nixon synthesis—the happy medium between the free market and price controls, between liberal trade and protectionism, between fiscal conservatism and big budget deficits, between laissez faire for business and subsidies or bailouts for particular companies and industries.

All these varieties of conservatism are bathed in a solvent of moral uplift and revolutionary rhetoric. This was the achievement of Mr. Nixon's 1971 State of the Union address, in which he declared that "the people of this nation are eager to get on with the quest for new greatness," affirmed that "it is for us here to open the doors that will set free again the real greatness of this nation—the genius of the American people," and called for a "New American Revolution . . . a revolution as profound, as far-reaching, as exciting, as that first revolution almost 200 years ago."

For those loyal Americans who feel the need for a somewhat more prosaic interpretation of the President's message, the following Revolutionist's Handbook and Pocket Companion may come in handy:

The Lift of a Driving Dream

The meaning of this concept is somewhat elusive, but one thing it clearly means is a surging economy. The GNP clock in the Commerce Department will tick faster, and there will be more real output and less inflation per tick.

But the dream itself—what will that be? Each man will have his own dream. The government will one day be out of the driving dream business.

Power to the People

Specifically, this means federal revenue-sharing with the states and cities. It also means tax cuts. But the concept of power to the people means more than revenue-sharing and tax cuts. It means a certain life style. It means youth-appeal. It means community control. It means a new revolution.

Fed Up with Government

"Let's face it," said the President. "Most Americans today are simply fed up with government at all levels."

That may sound like a contradiction to giving more power to governments at the state and local level. But state and local governments are closer to the people, so power is at least flowing in the right direction.

The Federal Government

After the New Revolution, we will still have a federal government. It will still have a large and vital role to play.

The federal government will still perform established functions that are clearly and essentially federal in nature. It will also acquire new functions—such as those urged by the President in welfare and health.

But the federal government will be completely reformed. Four Cabinet departments—State, Treasury, Defense, and Justice—will remain, but the eight others will become four— the Department of Economic Development, the Department of Community Development, the Department of Natural Resources, and the Department of Human Resources. You will get used to these titles. It will do you no good to go around muttering about George Orwell and 1984.

If a Cabinet officer doesn't like the name of his department, he can always ask to be head of a different department.

If we ever need another department, we can always make more, but the new revolutionary nomenclature really seems to have covered just about everything.

BUREAUCRACY

The New Revolution opposes the idea that a bureaucratic elite in Washington knows best what is best for people everywhere. We are going to get rid of the bureaucratic elite. Well, not exactly get rid of it, but put it in its place, peacefully downgrade it, and upgrade the people. "I have faith in the people," said the President.

Government at all levels must be refreshed and renewed and made truly responsive. In business terms, this seems to imply more consumerism, which would imply more controls on business.

On the other hand, since the New Revolution means less government *power*, perhaps business will be freer, after all. It is really too early to say.

PROSPERITY

The goal of the Revolution will be full prosperity in peacetime: more jobs, more income, more profits, without inflation and without war. Let's face it: Those are pretty controversial goals.

MONETARY POLICY

The independent Federal Reserve System will stay independent, but it has a new commitment. Its commitment is to provide fully for the monetary needs of a growing economy. It had darned well better live up to that commitment, or the President will rethink its independence.

FISCAL POLICY

We will achieve prosperity in part through a full-employment budget. By spending as if we were at full employment, we will help to create full employment.

Congress should accept the concept of the full-employment budget. It should not trouble itself about actual deficits, if they are presented in the President's budget.

But this is not to say that all deficits are a good thing. Deficits are very good if you have a full-employment surplus, but a full-employment deficit is very bad, especially if it results from congressional rather than presidential actions. Then it is inflationary.

To be sure, economists differ on just how to calculate the full-employment surplus and how to measure the degree of stimulation or restraint a given budget provides. Some economists even think actual full employment is more important than a full-employment surplus, but such economists are usually irresponsible New Dealers.

The full-employment-surplus concept provides the President with a definite basis for vetoing as inflationary any legislation he does not like if it exceeds his budget ceiling.

The New Revolution will be Republican.

MAXIMS FOR REVOLUTIONARIES

In the long, dark night of the American spirit, it is always seven o'clock in the morning.

*   *   *

All power to the blacks, ethnics, and Wasps.

*   *   *

The New Revolution will not hurt. It is bullish.

3. Blue-Collar Blues

There is a popular assumption in American politics that propertied interests are conservative and working-class interests are liberal. But President Nixon, while bearing the conservative banner, has never intended to concede the votes of trade unionists and other workers to his Democratic opponents. He has sensed that a great many working men are extremely conservative on social issues, such as the pace of movement of blacks into white neighborhoods, white schools, and white jobs. The most serious threat to Mr. Nixon's hopes of attracting labor support, however, has been whether he could stop inflation without a prolonged siege of unemployment.

Mr. Nixon wanted nothing so much as to throw off the Democratic charge that the Republicans are the party that brings depression and unemployment—the charge on which Democrats have been running ever since the Hoover Administration. The cruelest disappointment to the Nixon Administration was that slow monetary growth did not avoid a recession, did not avoid a rise in unemployment, and did not end the inflation.

Rising unemployment had worrisome side-effects; it greatly increased labor support for protection against foreign goods and aggravated neo-isolationist tendencies in the United States. In a rising economy, with jobs in different sectors plentiful, pressures for protectionism diminish, since labor can shift to where the good jobs are growing and out of the declining industries subject to low-wage import competition.

Rising unemployment has another side-effect that may be even more dangerous than protectionism in its implications for the national economy: It breeds resistance to cuts in defense expenditures. Since some of the biggest pockets of unemployment are found in states like Washington and California, where there have been defense cutbacks, and since it is hard for those laid-off workers—including many highly paid scientists, engineers, and other professionals—to find jobs in a tight labor market, pressures build up against reconversion to a peacetime economy.

It is vitally important to recognize that the unemployment problem resulting either from import competition or from defense cutbacks is essentially the same as the unemployment problem that was alleged to have resulted from automation in the early 1960's.

A torrid debate was waged at the start of the Kennedy Administration over whether automation—the faddist word used to describe any technological change that boosts productivity—would not breed mass unemployment. The

Kennedy Administration's economists insisted that in a rising economy more jobs would be created than improved technology would wipe out. They were right. Unemployment, which had reached 7 per cent at the start of 1961, fell below 4 per cent by early 1966, despite—or rather because of—an upsurge of investment in new plant and equipment. The automation issue, about which so many scare stories had been written by sociologists, engineers, and scientists as distinguished as Dr. Norbert Wiener, disappeared in the mid-1960's. But in the early 1970's, with rising unemployment, the automation issue re-emerged, together with opposition to foreign competition and to defense cutbacks.

Rising unemployment in the midst of inflation has also aggravated social tensions in the United States. Elements within the American labor movement today are becoming reactionary. During the great organizing drive of the American labor movement in the 1930's, blue-collar workers could say, with G. K. Chesterton,

> And we were angry and poor and happy,
> And proud of seeing our names in print.

Today, after three decades of economic growth, the workers' song should be rewritten to go,

> Still we are angry,
> But middle class and unhappy,
> And longing to see our names in print.

The blue-collar workers have become "forgotten Americans," and they want more attention paid to their grievances.

What is really bothering these blue-collar recruits to the middle class? And what can be done to ease their problems?

President George Meany of the AFL-CIO says that the "gut issue" is the pocketbook issue. Certainly the great majority of workers—like other Americans—feel that inflation is making them poorer, despite higher earnings.

But is it really so? Over-all data are misleading because they lump part-time and female labor together with full-time male workers, thereby dragging down the rate at which the average income of family breadwinners has been rising in the last five years. A special tabulation of census data prepared for Professor Sar Levitan of George Washington University shows that, since 1965, the average white married man employed in a blue-collar job has had a 15 per cent real increase in his annual income, measured in dollars of constant purchasing power. During the entire decade of the 1960's, white men in blue-collar jobs had real gains of 25 per cent—about the same as whites in all other occupations. With more wives working and more men moonlighting, family incomes of white workers rose still more dramatically during the 1960's. At the start of the decade, the income of white families headed by blue-collar workers aged 26 to 34 averaged $7,570 a year, measured in 1969 dollars. By the end of the decade, the average income of the same white families had gone up to $11,053—a real gain of 46 per cent.

But that gain in average family income, which lifted so many into the middle class, may have come at the cost of heightened personal and social strains. Moonlighting obviously is a source of tension, and so may be the increased entry of wives into the labor force. In 1960, only 33 per cent of the wives of white blue-collar workers held jobs. By 1970, this figure had risen to 44 per cent.

Another source of tension may have been the faster progress of blacks than whites in income and employment.

Measured in constant dollars, the annual income of black families headed by blue-collar workers aged 25 to 34 increased from $5,785 in 1960 to $9,494 in 1970—a gain of 64 per cent, compared with the 46 per cent increase of families headed by white workers in comparable jobs.

The gain of black and other nonwhite families in not just blue-collar but all occupations was even more rapid. From 1960 to 1970, all nonwhite families enjoyed a real increase in family income of 88 per cent, with annual earnings going up from $5,433 to $10,198. The wives of black workers were even more likely to be employed than those of whites. In 1960, 43 per cent of the wives of black workers held jobs; by 1970, this number had risen to 57 per cent.

Not only did blacks narrow the income gap during the 1960's, but they succeeded in increasing their share of blue-collar jobs, especially in manufacturing. Blacks increased the number of blue-collar jobs they held by 42 per cent during the decade, while whites gained only 7 per cent. To be sure, the total number of blue-collar jobs (what the census calls "operatives and craftsmen") held by whites was still 14.3 million in 1970, compared with 1.4 million held by nonwhites.

The narrowing of the income gap between whites and blacks undoubtedly bothered some whites. Relative income may be more important to the ego than absolute income. It is even possible that many white workers with more absolute income feel less secure after graduation to the middle class than they did before. They have taken on large debts. They have acquired homes and real estate that represent the largest share of their assets—and they fear huge losses of property values if there is "block-busting" and blacks move in.

Even more broadly, white workers who have moved up in the world are afraid of change that will wipe out the middle-class social values that they have struggled to achieve by working overtime at exhausting jobs, by moonlighting, by letting their wives go to work, and by going heavily into debt. This threat to their social values is what turns them so bitterly against demonstrating students, long-haired young people, and opponents of the Vietnam war (all of whom they tend to lump together). And this is why they try to wall themselves off in neighborhood enclaves.

What can be done about the economic and social grievances of these Middle Americans?

A Nixon Administration task force headed by Assistant Secretary of Labor Jerome M. Rosow suggested a long list of measures for helping blue-collar workers, including training programs to help them move up to better jobs: child-care services for their working wives, and not just for welfare mothers; more adult education in high schools and community colleges; government assistance to make it easier for their children to go to college; public relations programs, such as awards to workers and special postage stamps, to give more status to blue-collar jobs; more tax breaks for those in the $5,000 to $10,000 class. At the same time, the Rosow Task Force wanted to provide workers with more recreational facilities, such as vest-pocket parks, improved local transportation, improved disability protection, better housing, and other social benefits.

But that proposal and others like it have run up against one overwhelming obstacle: 40 per cent of all American families—including 70 million family members—have incomes between $5,000 and $10,000 a year. It is simply not possible to provide a significant increase in social benefits for 70 million people without increasing taxes—including the taxes they themselves must pay. If, as the Rosow report suggests, their taxes are to be cut, then the taxes of others must be raised still more.

Will such egalitarian policies be more successful in the future than they have been in the past? Professor Leonard Ross of the Columbia University Law School observes that, as a result of past efforts to redistribute income, to expand access of the middle class to public services, and to use tax exemptions for social purposes, the burden on the income tax has been multiplied, while its base has been contracted. "As the income tax became overloaded and unpopular," says Mr. Ross,

> liberal politicians turned to regressive payroll and consumption taxes to pay for the welfare state. Britain's pension system —financed largely by a highly regressive head tax—provides an illustration. In America, adoption of proposals for universal health insurance will compound the burden of the regressive payroll tax and increase pressure for a national sales tax (probably in the form of the European tax "on value added," a scheme already receiving friendly scrutiny in the Administration).

Certain specific programs may, of course, be targeted at the low end of the lower middle class. The Family Assistance Plan of the Nixon Administration, for instance, would help those just above the poverty line—the so-called working poor. But it cannot do much for the vast majority of the lower middle class. The costs of even a modest "negative income tax" to redistribute income would be enormous: Providing a minimum $3,600 income for a family of four would add $25 billion to the federal budget, and a $5,500 plan would cost $71 billion.

The problems of the working class cannot be solved in

isolation from those of the rest of the nation, including economic stagnation, inflation, and the strains of rapid social change. The blues of blue-collar workers are the blues of America. Unable to cope with those complex national problems, every group seeks to protect itself—when it can—by the use of such monopoly power as it may possess. Thus some labor unions, such as those in the construction trades, seek to restrict access of black workers to jobs, and white families in some neighborhoods seek to restrict the access of black families to housing or schools. But the splits in the American society are widened and its tensions exacerbated by such recourse to monopoly power. A major responsibility of government is to check the abuse of private monopoly power in order to defend minority rights.

4. The Enterprise System

Monopoly in industrial markets, as well as in labor markets, poses a serious problem for the conservative hoping to minimize government intervention in the private economy. The Nixon Administration has not been able to avoid the horns of the classic dilemma of whether the modern industrial economy needs more rather than less planning and control, or more vigorous antitrust prosecution and more competition.

Antitrust is, as the historian Richard Hofstadter put it, "one of the faded passions of American reform." Still, antitrust retains a place in the American myth: Liberals can support it because they retain their old suspicion of business behavior, and conservatives because they still believe in competition and may hope to gain an additional point of leverage in the battle against inflation. The broad public accepts and may even like bigness (in an age of television, mass communications, and anonymity, it apparently prefers big corporations whose names it can recognize). Periodically, however, a story breaks—such as the electrical price-fixing case—that reawakens public distrust of big-business behavior and regenerates support for antitrust action. This has again been done by Ralph Nader and his team of young investigators who, in their 1,148-page report, "The Closed Enterprise System," present some intriguing cases, such as these:

• Between 1953 and 1961, a hundred tablets of the antibiotic drug tetracycline retailed for about $51.00. This price was set collusively by some of the nation's biggest pharmaceutical companies. Ten years later, after the exposure of congressional hearings and indictment of some companies under the antitrust laws, the price of tetracycline for the same quantity was cut to about $5.00, a 90 per cent decrease.

• In the early 1960's, an international cartel cornered the world market in quinine, which is taken mostly by old people to restore their natural heart rhythm. The price of quinine was boosted from 37 cents an ounce to $2.13.

• In 1964, the price of bread in the United States averaged 20 cents a loaf. In Seattle, a local price-fixing conspiracy set the price at 24 cents. When a Federal Trade Commission ruling ended the conspiracy, the Seattle price began to decline and reached the national average in 1966. During the ten years of the price conspiracy, however, consumers in the Seattle-Tacoma area paid an estimated $35 million extra for bread.

• In the early 1960's, nearly all of the country's manufacturers of plumbing fixtures met secretly and decided to produce only the most expensive sinks and toilets, charging uniformly high prices. Consumers had to purchase the "Cadillac" of plumbing fixtures.

None of these cases cited by the Nader group would have surprised Adam Smith, who distrusted cooperation among businessmen as much as he did government regulation of business; he warned of "the mean rapacity, the monopolizing spirit of merchants and manufacturers, who neither are nor ought to be the rulers of mankind." Foes of government intervention in the economy, however, characteristically ignore or underrate the damage to public interest of private monopoly.

Businessmen in America rarely attempt to justify price-fixing—at least publicly—or attack the antitrust laws in principle. As Hofstadter put it:

> Visitations by the Department of Justice are a nuisance, lawsuits are expensive, and prosecution carries an unpleasant stigma, but the antitrust procedures can be considered an alternative to more obtrusive regulation, such as outright controls on prices. At any rate, big business has never found it necessary or expedient to launch a public campaign against antitrust enforcement; the pieties at stake are too deep to risk touching.

However, where concentration of industry is concerned, rather than a price conspiracy, most businessmen refuse to accept the idea that antitrust and antimerger actions serve consumer interests.

The Nader report offers cases to show the costs to consumers of market concentration. For instance, it mentions a case of market concentration in Duluth-Superior, where three big milk companies accounted for more than 90 per cent of all the milk sold. By contrast, in Minneapolis–St. Paul, there was a large number of competing milk firms, and it was easy for new firms to enter the market. Despite similar production and distribution costs for milk in the two markets, the wholesale price of a half-gallon of milk in 1967 was 33.8 cents in Minneapolis–St. Paul and 45 cents in Duluth-Superior, a 33 per cent difference.

The report also notes that, in the mid–1960's, most university students were paying 25 cents a page to have their papers reproduced on copying machines. As competition among sellers grew, the price fell to 2 cents to 5 cents per page. The service became faster, and the machines more conveniently located.

Champions of highly concentrated markets argue that the great size of corporations produces many efficiencies and encourages technological innovation. But the Nader group maintains that the reputed efficiencies of large-scale operations are overrated and become inefficiencies when the scale grows too large.

Most economists nowadays contend that economies of size are frequently outweighed by the greater efficiency that results from sharp market competition. Their view is that competition is also a spur to technological innovation. This position is documented in a study, *Technological Change in Regulated Industries,* edited by Associate Dean William M. Capron of the Kennedy School of Government at Harvard University and published by the Brookings Institution. The over-all conclusion of the study was that competition should be increased even in the regulated industries as a stimulant to technological advancement. In the Capron volume, William G. Shepherd of the University of Michigan urges the Federal Communications Commission to seek ways to introduce competition into certain parts of the telecommunications industry—for instance, in the large-scale transmission of data, use of domestic satellites as alternatives to land-based transmission, and supply of telecommunications equipment.

Almarin Phillips of the University of Pennsylvania finds that the Civil Aeronautics Board, by legalizing a price-fixing monopoly, has diverted competition in the airlines to nonprice factors, including not only speed or convenience but in-flight amenities. Price-fixing regulation of the airlines has bred excess capacity and low profits.

Aaron J. Gellman of the Budd Company and the University of Pennsylvania concludes that the Interstate Commerce Commission, through minimum-rate regulation, has stifled innovation in surface freight transportation by denying carriers the right to reduce rates when new low-cost equipment is introduced. Gellman argues that innovative performance in the transport industry can best be improved by gradually eliminating regulation and by encouraging intermodal-transportation firms to develop.

Reportedly, the Nixon Administration is toying with the idea of deregulating transportation. However, some economists are worried that the Administration might deregulate only transportation prices and rates, but not entry. The economists fear that if tight and highly concentrated market structures are preserved, the deregulation of prices would hurt rather than benefit consumers and transportation-users, since a monopolistic market would be preserved.

It is significant that as the economists, both liberal and conservative, move back toward Adam Smith in their respect for competition, the young lawyers are heading back to Louis Brandeis and the trustbusting movement. The Nader report lays down some rough guidelines to prevent concentrations of economic power. It would break up oligopolistic industries—defined as industries in which four firms supply more than 50 per cent or eight firms more than 70 per cent of the relevant market; it would ban further mergers by the top 500 industrial corporations, unless they spin off assets equal to a merger; and it would impose an absolute limit of $2 billion on the assets of any corporation except utilities and rate-regulated industries. The aim would be not only to increase economic efficiency but also to reduce the political power of great corporations—which Mr. Nader charges the corporations use to shield themselves from government regulation on environmental pollution, to extract subsidies and benefits from the taxpayers, and to gain shelter from foreign competition. A prime example cited by the Nader group is oil import quotas, which, according to estimates of the Nixon Administration's Cabinet Task Force on Oil Import Control, are costing American consumers between $5 billion and $8 billion a year. Unfortunately, Mr. Nixon tabled the report, prepared under the chairmanship of George P. Shultz, and rejected its recommendation that oil import quotas be replaced by a less costly tariff system.

The issue of monopoly power and performance has continuously plagued the Nixon Administration. The most dramatic business event of recent years, the collapse of the Penn Central Railroad, shattered once and for all the notion that bigness assures either efficiency or technological progress. Penn Central may seem like an exceptional case, but, unfortunately, the same lesson could be read in aerospace, the airlines, electric power, and other fields, such as steel. Indeed, it was the steel industry, more than any other, that forced the Nixon Administration to abandon its policy of staying out of industrial wage-and-price decision-making.

In January of 1971, there was a confrontation between the Nixon Administration and the steel industry. The confrontation ended when Bethlehem cut its price hike on structural steel from 12 per cent to 6.8 per cent, matching U.S. Steel's increase.

Until U.S. Steel came through with its lower price-hike, undercutting Bethlehem's, the Nixon Administration spent many anxious hours trying to decide what it would do if the whole steel industry held firm with Bethlehem, despite the President's use of the jawbone that he had so often denounced and had declared he would not use.

Mr. Nixon's jawboning was built on the threat of using one of the two principal market weapons he had in his possession. One would have been a drastic reduction or elimination of steel import quotas. Mr. Nixon sought to make this threat credible by having the State Department cancel a negotiating session in Frankfurt, West Germany, to work out a new steel import quota agreement. The second threat was to withhold government contracts from steel producers who boosted prices as much as Bethlehem had done. But, if the steel industry stuck together, the government would have had to fill its steel needs from abroad— or escalate the pressure by taking really rough antitrust action against the steel industry.

Steel industry leaders were strongly tempted to try to outface the Administration. Bethlehem Steel and Allen Wood Steel dug in for what they expected might be a long siege. They simply did not believe that the government was willing to break the steel industry's resistance by letting in masses of foreign steel. They kept asking, "Does America want to have a steel industry or not?" They thought the price in balance-of-payments losses and rising unemployment would be too high for the Administration to pay, either economically or politically.

The Administration was only too aware of the dangers of resorting to massive retaliation. "Everyone here knows steel is in poor shape," said one Administration official in the midst of the crisis. But the Nixon team could simply not let Bethlehem's "enormous," as the President's press secretary called it, price-hike stand. It would have fed into the cost structure of many other industries, and would have caused the United Steel Workers to raise their wage demands still higher.

The timing of Bethlehem's 12 per cent hike was bad from Mr. Nixon's standpoint; it came on the same day the Administration announced a generous liberalization of depreciation allowances, which gave business a tax reduction of approximately $4 billion a year. A President seeking to polish up his reputation with all sectors of the society did not want to seem to be a patsy for business. Was this the steel industry's response to his plea for "special restraint," which he had made before the National Association of Manufacturers? Thus, it seemed to the President and his advisers that Mr. Nixon's credibility was at stake.

The drama began with the Administration in a seemingly passive mood. When Bethlehem's Chairman Stewart S. Cort discussed the planned price changes with Dr. Paul W. McCracken, the President's chief economist, on Monday, January 11, 1971, several hours before the increases were made public, Mr. Cort gained the impression that Dr. McCracken, though not enthusiastic over the price hike, "did not seem excessively disturbed."

After Dr. McCracken's session with Mr. Cort, a spokesman for the Council of Economic Advisers said that there had been no change in the Administration's policy of re-

fraining from comment on individual price actions. On
Tuesday, January 12, with this reaffirmation of the Administration's hands-off policy published in the morning news-
papers, came the President's blast against Bethlehem from
San Clemente, California. It was Mr. Nixon's first out-and-
out use of the jawbone.

What had happened? Had the President in San Clemente
overruled his economic advisers in Washington? Had his
politicos decided to take over?

On the contrary, the advice to the President to blast
Bethlehem's 12 per cent price hike came from the same
group of economists in Washington—including Budget Director George Shultz, Chairman Paul McCracken, and C.E.A.
member Herbert Stein—who had been the President's closest
consultants on wage-price policy all along.

Mr. Nixon and his aides were not at all sure of how far
they wanted to carry the new activism, because they were
troubled over three basic dilemmas. The first was a dilemma
of principle. The Nixon Administration still did not like to
use government power to determine private price-and-wage
decisions. It felt that this distorts business judgment and the
proper allocation of resources. Yet, during the confrontation
with the steel industry, the Administration came to recognize that it may not be wise to trust all price- and wage-
setting to industrial monopolies and oligopolies, especially
when they are the recipient of special government protection. "Steel is hardly a perfect model of free price competition," said one Administration policy-maker during the
crisis.

The second dilemma was political. The Administration
originally preferred to keep its mouth shut and to act—if at
all—through its impact on the market. But to improve the
structure of markets by reforms of the kind recommended by

Chairman Arthur F. Burns of the Federal Reserve Board could be extremely time-consuming and politically unpopular, especially with some of the Administration's most important supporters. How easy would it be, for instance, for the Administration to invoke a major liberalization of oil import quotas? What would be the political cost of markedly more vigorous enforcement of the antitrust laws? Could the Administration get legislation for compulsory arbitration of labor disputes that involve the public interest? Could it get Congress to enact national building codes to break down the barriers for adopting modern production techniques in the construction industry? The one item on Dr. Burns's list of industrial reforms, which he spelled out in a speech at Pepperdine College, that the Administration rushed to accomplish was, in fact, the liberalization of depreciation allowances for business, and this was not precisely a get-tough approach to business.

The third dilemma troubling the Nixon Administration was that, even if it were willing to pay the political price of a much tougher policy to reform the structure of industry and labor unions and to curb inflationary wage-and-price hikes, would it really accomplish much in improving the trade-off between inflation and unemployment? Would there be a heavy penalty through more strikes and longer strikes? But, on the other side, if the Administration did not get tougher, was there a chance that wage-and-price inflation would again accelerate rather than recede as the economy was stimulated by faster monetary growth and tax cuts? This, too, would bear a heavy price for the Nixon Administration.

Thus, there remained grave uncertainties as to how far the Nixon Administration's advisers thought it should go toward a more activist wage-and-price policy. They adopted what they called a "nontheological" approach. This involved some movement away from the President's initial position that he would not "jawbone" business or labor or put pressure on them to keep prices and wages down.

As the result of the unexpected concatenation of business recession, rising unemployment, and continuing inflation, the profits of corporations and the real income of working men had been depressed. Businessmen, trying to offset falling profits, boosted prices if they had the market power to do so. Workers, trying to make up for the inroads of inflation and fewer working hours, used their power in the market to get bigger wage gains.

To curb monopoly power in labor and product markets, the Administration began marching under the flag of a "new pragmatism." Pragmatism is the philosophy that postulates that what works is the test of what's good. The virtue of the philosophy is that it is a strong antidote to rigid ideology; its fault is that it may become a rationalization for mere opportunism. But, after the steel confrontation, the Nixon Administration knew it was running out of time for sticking to its initial principles.

The objective fact was that, despite the semi-rollback of structural steel prices, the steel industry had boosted its prices by 7 per cent, had held open the door for further price increases, and had warded off a threat to its "voluntary" import quotas, which shield it from foreign competition.

Thus, the logic of economic history was inexorably moving the Nixon Administration toward price controls. If the Administration would do little or nothing to break up oligopolies to force greater price competition, and if it refused to expose an industry like steel to greater foreign competition, then it had no choice but to curb the abuse of market power by corporations and labor unions.

The need to impose wage-and-price restraints was intensified as the Nixon Administration moved to provide stronger fiscal stimulus to restore the economy to full employment. In the face of persistent inflation, Mr. Nixon was prepared to accept big and growing budget deficits. But he had to reconcile these deficits with traditional Republican fiscal conservatism.

5. The Full-Employment Budget

In the wake of President Nixon's statement that, although his budget for fiscal 1973 would be in deficit—by $25 billion, after deficits of $39 billion in fiscal 1972 and $23 billion in 1971—government expenditures would not exceed "full-employment" revenues, there was a spreading wave of confusion and skepticism on the part of many people who refused to believe that there was any such thing as a full-employment budget, and who feared that the President was simply playing games with them. One such skeptic was Virginia Blivis of West Egg, L.I., who wrote:

Dear Economic Specialist:
Somehow I don't see how the federal budget can be in deficit and still not be in deficit at the same time. The Presi-

dent used to say that he would balance the federal budget so I can balance my family budget. The federal budget is not in balance and neither is my family budget, even though my husband is fully employed.

My husband says the President is just being political and there is no such thing as a full-employment surplus. My husband says I should write to you and ask whether I should believe the President. I know if you say it in the *Times,* it is so.

[signed]
VIRGINIA BLIVIS, age 43.

The reply was:

Dear Virginia:
Your husband is wrong.

Yes, Virginia, there is a full-employment surplus, and I am going to tell you what it is. But this is going to take a little time, so you must be patient and attentive.

The President has learned a lot since he said he must balance his budget so every family could balance its budget. It is essentially the other way around. Right now, the President is right in saying he must *unbalance* his budget so more families can balance theirs—that is, get more income to offset their outgo. That is especially true for people who, unlike your husband, are out of work.

To explain the full-employment surplus, Virginia, I must first tell you about functions. A function is a relationship between one thing that changes and another thing that changes. Nobody has ever seen a function, but we all know that they exist, just as we know that there is love and beauty in the world.

The more the rain falls, the more the grass grows; that is a function. The more calories you consume, the fatter you get; that is also a function.

And, Virginia, the more gross national product grows, the more taxes flow into the United States Treasury. That is a tax function. Since we have a progressive tax system, tax collections rise faster than rising income. And, vice versa, when income is falling, tax collections fall off faster still.

Thus, our tax system is what we call a built-in stabilizer, Virginia. It slows down increases in people's spendable income when business climbs, and it also slows down the drop in spendable income when business slumps.

Just keep thinking of that tax function, Virginia, though you cannot see it.

There is also an expenditure function. It is a built-in stabilizer, too. The *more* gross national product rises in a given year, the *less* the government will spend, because there will be fewer people out of work collecting unemployment compensation or other social benefits. But if GNP slumps, the more the government must spend to help the unemployed, the farmers who are hit by falling prices, and the people who are going onto relief or taking early retirement.

As a result of rising taxes and lower government expenditures when the economy is booming and we move up to full employment, the federal budget runs a surplus. But when the economy slumps and unemployment grows, taxes drop, government spending rises, and the federal budget slides into deficit.

That is the situation now. Unemployment nearly is 6 per cent, and the federal budget for fiscal year 1973 will show a $25 billion deficit.

But if we were at full employment, which most economists define as 4 per cent unemployment, the budget would be in surplus. We don't really know what the surplus would be, but the Administration's estimate is that the full-employment surplus would be $700 million.

What budget policy should we follow to reduce unemployment?

Basically we have three choices:

• Switch to a tighter budget—that is, one with a full-employment surplus greater than $700 million.

• Stand pat on the $700 million full-employment surplus budget.

• Switch to a more stimulative budget—that is, one with a full-employment surplus lower than $700 million.

The first step is the worst. A tighter budget would aggravate unemployment. It would do this by reducing spendable income at every level of GNP.

President Hoover committed this blunder of going for a tighter budget—by raising taxes and cutting spending—when the economy was sliding into the Depression. He seriously aggravated the Depression.

The second course—standing pat on the existing budget—is better. It at least permits the tax function and the expenditure function to act as built-in stabilizers. They slow the decline of income and employment.

The third course—switching to a looser budget—is probably the best of all. Some combination of tax cuts and government-expenditure hikes will increase spendable income at every level of GNP. More spending for goods and services will mean more jobs.

This will not do much about inflation, however. Nobody is perfect, Virginia.

Economists will quarrel a great deal about the President's new budget—what things he is spending money on, what taxes he is cutting, what forecast of the economy he is making, what inflation he is assuming, how his economists estimate the full-employment surplus, whether the budget is too stimulative or too restrictive.

But what is important is that economists will hail the President for accepting the full-employment budget concept. He will not do the wrong thing, like President Hoover, trying to balance the budget with lots of unemployment. He will not just sit there on his built-in stabilizers. No, he will shift the tax and expenditure functions and reduce the full-employment surplus. That is his policy of activism.

So don't believe your husband, Virginia. Though, down here, we are deep in deficit, somewhere up there, out near the end of the tax and expenditure functions, there really is a full-employment surplus. Like the President, we must go on believing in it. It will live in the minds and hearts of economists eternally, or at least for several more editions of the standard economics textbooks.

[signed]
Your friend,
Economic Specialist

6. Toward an Incomes Policy

The Nixon Administration's progress toward an incomes policy moved a millimeter at a time. More than a year before the wage-price freeze in 1971, the President had appointed a Productivity Commission and called upon his Council of Economic Advisers to issue periodic "inflation alerts." However, the first inflation alert, issued in August, 1970, did not send anyone running for the bomb shelter. Chairman Paul W. McCracken had told the press that he thought "there is some evidence that after a long period here we are beginning to see some things shaping up in the price area that gives some hope that we are going to make some real progress in the period ahead." Was Dr. McCracken's optimism not shaken by Ford's announcement of a price increase on both cars and trucks? No, he replied, his optimism was based on the totality of evidence. Within that total picture, however, he knew there would be disappointments along the way.

Then was the Ford announcement a disappointment? Of course, said the chairman of the Council, news of a price increase "is not a leading candidate for the best news of the day." But he had not examined the Ford data in detail, and he would have no comment to make on the specific issue.

However, Dr. McCracken had since met quietly in Detroit with top auto industry officials.

The inflation alert made no reference whatsoever to the wage negotiation in the auto industry—that was the most crucial economic issue immediately ahead. This was no careless omission.

Dr. McCracken emphasized that the alert "never was intended to be some kind of anticipation exercise." In its first report, the Council of Economic Advisers was alerting the public to some historical trends. It also called attention to certain specific developments in metals, metal products, fuels and power, pulp, paper and allied products, nonmetallic mineral products, trucking, cigarettes, rubber tires, and electric power. But the report strongly implied that cigarette and tire companies, in increasing their prices faster than their costs were rising, had done something questionable.

What did Dr. McCracken expect to happen as a result of the analysis of these areas? He hoped that the Council would thereby succeed in lifting the "level of visibility and understanding and awareness of these complex developments in the price-cost area"—and that, as a result, "in the inscrutable way that these do, they can start to have some impact on public policy."

That sounded more militant. Did it mean, for instance, that the Council of Economic Advisers would warn the

Productivity Commission that oil quotas were having an inflationary effect and that the government should switch to an oil tariff system?

No, said Dr. McCracken, the Productivity Commission "is not concerned with this at all." Rather, it is concerned with basic forces determining longer-run trends in productivity.

However, he added, the Domestic Council would be looking into the question of whether the nation might be running into a shortage of fuel oil this winter. Dr. McCracken was chairman of the subcommittee of the Domestic Council that would be looking into this matter.

What other effects, then, would the inflation alerts have on public policy?

The key word to remember, Dr. McCracken insisted, was "inscrutable." "I said that I would hope that this can be factored into public consideration and discussions," he said, "and that these in that inscrutable way will help create a better understanding of a problem and thus can start to make an impact on public policy."

Waxing eloquent, he declared, "I think that is basic to our kind of democracy, that the more there is understanding of the problem, the better our public policy decisions are going to be. And this is fundamentally the contribution we hope this thing could make."

What better public policies did he want?

By better policies, Dr. McCracken said, he meant "more policies that will enable us to come closer to having full employment, vigorous economic growth, and a stable price level. How is that?"

At this point in the press conference, there was laughter, as deeper understanding suddenly arrived.

The press might have spared itself much agony and confusion if it had read the passage of the first inflation alert that stated: "The important point is that the explanation of inflation cannot be found, or the blame for it assigned, by looking at the behavior of particular prices, or categories of prices, although this behavior is significant for many other purposes and most of this report is devoted to describing it."

The economic theory of the President's Council of Economic Advisers, in a nutshell, was that inflation is caused by inappropriate monetary and fiscal policies and that the market power of particular corporations or unions has nothing to do with it.

A rise in the price of Product A, it asserted, may simply mean that consumers will have less money to spend on products B, C, D, E, and so on.

If this is not the case, the President's economists wanted to know, "where do consumers get the money to increase their total spending?"

The implication was that no individual wage or price action can have any effect on general inflation, which only the government or the Federal Reserve can cause.

Economists who disagreed with this line of reasoning would reply that, if the Administration were unwilling to countenance high unemployment, and if corporations and unions were pushing up their prices and wages, enough money would have to be fed into the system to support those inflationary price-and-wage decisions.

The first inflation alert did, however, make one remarkable contribution to the theory of inflation. It asserted that the longer an inflation lasts, the harder it is to end it. Since the preceding year and a half of the inflation had occurred during the Nixon Administration, this might have been taken as a self-indictment for its policy of gradualism. However, that was apparently water under the dam, because the inflation was slowly dying, although Dr. McCracken refused to forecast consumer prices for 1970 as a whole.

The position of the Council of Economic Advisers, disclosed in this first inflation alert, was that an inflation, once set in motion, must be permitted to work its way through the economic system. "Wholesale prices begin rising first, followed by retail and service prices and wages. This process has to run through the system before a leveling off can occur."

The inflation alert made it clear that the Nixon Administration had no intention of confessing error in having given business and labor a green light to raise prices and wages without concern about government resistance when Mr. Nixon took office in January, 1969. It held to this line as inflation escalated through 1969. Nor did it see any need to change its laissez-faire policy in 1970.

Thus, the new inflation alert and Productivity Commission, which were created by the Nixon Administration in response to growing demands that it do something to restrain wages and prices, recalled Mort Sahl's classic distinction between old-fashioned and modern conservatives: The former believed you should never do anything for the first time; the latter believed that you should do things for the first time—but not now.

So the inflation dragged on. In mid-summer of 1971, Chairman Burns of the Federal Reserve Board declared, "The rules of economics are not working in quite the way they used to." Coming from the economics profession's "great pragmatist," this was distressing news. It was like an explorer's discovering that, in the vicinity of the North Pole, his compass spun around and pointed south-southwest instead of north. The particular rule Dr. Burns had in mind

was, of course, the one that goes: "An increase in the slack
in the economy and in unemployment will cause a slowdown
in inflation." That rule was the basis of the Nixon Administration's Game Plan I, that lasted from Inauguration Day,
January 20, 1969, through Election Day, November 3, 1970,
when the Republicans lost ground in Congress and state-
houses around the country.

The rule has a corollary that goes, "Persistent slack in the
economy, even with unemployment shrinking, will cause
inflation to evaporate." This was the basis of Game Plan
II, which called for economic recovery based primarily on
a more rapid increase in the money supply—but without an
incomes policy to restrain prices and wages. Dr. Burns did
not think Game Plan II was working out; that's why he
kept calling for an incomes policy, which seemed to get
tougher every time he mentioned it. Dr. Burns apparently
had grown more and more convinced that the inflation
would not respond to what economists call macroeconomic
policy—that is, over-all monetary and fiscal policy—because
of changes in the way the economic system is working.

The basic unemployment rule behind game plans I and II
depended upon two propositions:

• That, with slack in the economy, competition would intensify and businessmen would stiffen their resistance to excessive wage demands.

• That, with unemployment high, workers would work
harder and reduce their wage demands lest employers seek
to cut costs by laying off still more workers—and replace
them with lower paid people from "the reserve army of the
unemployed."

Thus, as wage gains slowed and productivity rose, cost
pressures on employers would abate and inflation would
vanish.

The Administration continued to contend that these propositions remained valid. Its economists insisted that their game plan had worked, although, they admitted, less well than they had expected—with somewhat more unemployment and somewhat less progress against inflation.

Dr. Burns disagreed. He found little or no evidence of progress against inflation, and he sounded worried that events might be moving the other way.

In testimony before the Joint Economic Committee, he said that an adjusted measure of wages rose a bit more in the first half of 1971 than in the previous two years. "This sustained sharp rise in wages during a period of substantial economic slack," said Dr. Burns, "contrasts markedly with our experience in earlier recessions, when the rate of advance in wages typically dropped sharply or actually ceased."

What was behind the change?

Some economists think it has been a change in the structure of the labor force. Dr. George Perry of the Brookings Institution notes that there are more female and young workers, aged sixteen to twenty-four, than there used to be. Since these groups have higher unemployment rates than "prime"-age men—that is, between the ages of twenty-four and sixty-five—there is less slack in the labor force and more pressure on wage rates than there used to be at any given over-all rate of unemployment.

But other economists contend the problem is basically one of inflationary expectations on the part of both labor and management. Workers expect prices to go on shooting up, so they demand more. Employers expect prices to go on climbing, so they are more willing to give on the wage side.

Professor Ronald I. McKinnon of Stanford University holds that the crucial change is in management's lack of resistance; he contends that labor is pushing on an open door.

The reason, he says, is that business sees the rapid growth of the money supply and expects that the Federal Reserve and the Administration will continue to put enough money into the economy to prevent serious unemployment. Hence, business executives see little point in fighting hard, being willing to hold out against long strikes, possibly jeopardizing the very existence of their businesses in order to resist an inflationary wage demand; they prefer to grant the wage increase and pass it on to consumers via price increases.

This logic is not necessarily inconsistent with Dr. Perry's findings on the changed structure of the labor force. High-employment policies, in all Western industrial societies, draw more females and young workers into the labor force. They also bring about faster rural-urban migration, increasing the number of uneducated and low-skilled workers looking for industrial jobs.

In the United States, rapid social change—and changing social attitudes—may be aggravating inflation, as blue-collar workers show more intransigence and militance in a society where they feel like outsiders. Hostility on the part of white workers toward blacks and other minorities breeds indifference toward unemployment, which is much more heavily concentrated among the minority groups.

As in the society generally, there is less respect for authority—not only that of employers but that of trade union leaders as well. Union bargainers, even striving to be "responsible," are afraid to have the workers throw moderate settlements back in their faces.

It is possible that slow economic growth and moderate unemployment, instead of damping down wage demands, may even work perversely, because employed workers, with less overtime pay, periodic layoffs, and climbing living costs, are more determined than ever to get extra big increases in

wage rates to keep their real annual take-home pay from declining.

Administration stalwarts in July, 1971, still talked hope-
fully that in the coming months inflation would nevertheless
prove to be slowing down, even as the economy advanced.
But the money supply had increased rapidly and the budget
was sliding deeper into deficit; there was reason to fear that
these would add to inflation and endanger the recovery, because interest rates were climbing and businessmen and consumers were jittery. Unemployment was sticking around 6
per cent. Internationally, the dollar was weakening—partly
as a consequence of persistent inflation. Time had finally
run out on Mr. Nixon's old game plans I and II, which were
first cousins.

7. The New Economic Policy

President Nixon launched his New Economic Policy on August 15, 1971, and called it the most comprehensive economic program since President Roosevelt's New Deal.

The Roosevelt and Nixon reformations could not have been more different. The New Deal came at a time of drastically falling prices; Mr. Nixon's N.E.P. (not to be confused with Lenin's N.E.P., which represented the overhaul of the Soviet economic game plan of the early 1920's) came in the midst of inflation. General Hugh S. Johnson used to denounce price-"chiselers"—that is, price-cutters; Secretary of the Treasury John B. Connally has attacked price-"gougers" —or price-raisers.

The New Deal spawned a school of new government agencies—the Federal Deposit Insurance Corporation, the Social

Security System, the Fair Labor Standards Act, the Securities and Exchange Commission, the National Labor Relations Board, the Public Works Administration, the Works Progress Administration, the Federal Housing Administration, and many others, some of which are still alive and kicking, and others of which are long since gone and all but forgotten.

The New Economic Policy, at the outset, fathered only one creature—the Cost of Living Council—pronounced "coke" for short, because it was intended to provide the pause that refreshes. This was later to be augmented by the Pay Board and the Price Commission and a few lesser committees.

Where the New Deal greatly expanded the role of government (said F.D.R., "we will spend and spend, tax and tax, elect and elect"), Mr. Nixon hoped to shrink the role of government—by cutting taxes, especially on business, by postponing or cutting government expenditures, and by laying off federal workers to offset the impact of the tax cut.

Yet there are a few similarities as well. Mr. Roosevelt devalued the dollar, and Mr. Nixon did the same. Perhaps the most striking similarity between the New Deal and the New Economic Policy was the vigorous effort at rebuilding public confidence. Mr. Roosevelt's most famous sentence was, "We have nothing to fear but fear itself." Earlier, Mr. Nixon had sought to build confidence by issuing, with the help of his staff, cheerful readings of economic indicators, but as the indicators stayed sour or went still more sour, he finally became activist with a vengeance. Like Mr. Roosevelt, Mr. Nixon decided to build confidence not by Hooverian reassurances that prosperity is just around the corner but by "looking busy."

In retrospect, it can be said that Mr. Roosevelt's program,

on the fundamental issue of fiscal policy, was rather modest, for the New Deal increased government spending by sums that, even in relation to GNP, we would now consider small. At the same time, Roosevelt foolishly increased taxes in an effort to offset spending increases. Similarly, Mr. Nixon's fiscal policy did not look remarkably stimulative; he asked for some expenditure cuts to offset his proposed tax cuts.

Yet Mr. Nixon's fiscal policy provided a shot in the arm for the economy. With the Democrats in Congress helping to push for bigger spending programs and tax reductions, fiscal policy under the N.E.P. proved to be more stimulative than the President originally said he wanted. His international moves were fundamentally designed to stimulate American exports and boost the sales of import-competing American industries. But his most important single action was probably the demonstration that the Administration was willing to attack inflation. Imposing a freeze on wages and prices dramatized the President's anti-inflation policy and forced it deeply into the consciousness of consumers, workers, and businessmen. The country had been longing for action, and it was relieved when action finally came.

Monetary growth slowed down as inflationary expectations declined and the demand for cash of business diminished. In terms of dollars, gross national product kept growing as fast as it had before—but, with inflation under better control, the biggest gains were coming in real output and real income.

When Congress reassembled in September, 1971, and confronted Mr. Nixon's New Economic Policy, with its wage-price freeze, tax cuts, import surcharge, and floating dollar, the Democrats found themselves in that state of mind once vividly described by Anthony Trollope:

It was the injustice of the thing that rankled so deeply. . . . It was as when a player is checkmated by some audacious combination of two pawns and a knight, such being all the remaining forces of the victorious adversary, when the beaten man has two castles and a queen upon the board. It was, indeed, worse than this—for the adversary had appropriated to his own use the castles and the queen of the unhappy vanquished one. . . . This man, this audacious Cagliostro among statesmen, this destructive leader of all declared Conservatives, had come forward without a moment's warning, and pretended that he would do the thing out of hand!

The passage is from Trollope's novel *Phineas Redux,* published in 1873; it describes the way British Liberals felt when the Conservative leader, Mr. Daubeny, beat them to the punch on church reform—that is, on the disestablishment of the Church of England. This was as shocking a turnabout for the Conservatives a century ago as the freezing of wages and prices and the severing of the bond between the dollar and gold were for the Republicans in 1971.

Mr. Nixon, like the fictional Mr. Daubeny, had appropriated the policies of his political opponents. But the critical question remained, "Will it work?"

The Democrats could conceivably have tried to prevent Mr. Nixon's program from working by denying it their support in Congress. But Mr. Nixon had swung into action, because, as Trollope's shrewd political analyst, St. Bungay, put it, "he can do it, and we can't. He will get from our side much support, and we should get none from his."

Despite their unhappiness, the Democrats were compelled to back Mr. Nixon on the freeze and the Phase Two incomes policy that followed it. They did not press the President to end the float of the dollar or to prop gold back on its throne. They did not oppose a devaluation of the dollar in relation to other currencies.

Liberal traders in both parties inveighed against the 10 per cent border tax on imports, but there was enough protectionist sentiment in Congress to support the President's use of the tax as a bargaining weapon, until he was able to get the currency realignment he wanted.

To be sure, liberals on the Democratic side attacked Mr. Nixon's fiscal priorities, arguing that his tax-cut proposals were unfairly balanced on the side of big business. But the Democrats gave the Republican President essentially the tax bill he asked for.

As originally conceived, Mr. Nixon's N.E.P. was designed to provide the major thrust to the economy not just by tax cuts but also by wage-and-price controls and by the dollar devaluation. Blocking inflation and ending inflationary expectations were expected to unleash a great increase in consumer spending. The Administration expected that consumers, whose saving rate had been running more than a third higher than normal, would pour billions extra into the economy. This would help jazz up business investment in new plant and equipment, with a 7 per cent investment tax credit to provide an extra push. The Administration also was determined to hang onto its new rules for fast write-offs of capital equipment, worth about $4 billion a year. The total tax cuts to business totaled $8 billion—and those to consumers $1 billion.

Realignment of the dollar with other currencies was another economic needle for the domestic economy. American economists are so much in the habit of comparing net exports to gross national product that they sometimes underrate the size and potential power of a dollar devaluation.

United States merchandise exports and imports were each running in excess of $45 billion in 1971. If, by the combination of currency changes and trade actions, the Administration were able to add 10 per cent to U.S. exports, this would add $4.5 billion to GNP. And, if imports were scaled down by 10 per cent, this would add $4.5 billion to sales of U.S. goods that are import substitutes.

A total increase of $9 billion from international monetary and trade moves would be precisely as stimulative as a $9 billion tax cut or expenditure increase.

But neither the stimulus from a big swing in the U.S. foreign trade balance nor one from a rapid climb in consumer and business spending could be counted on as being in the bag.

The gains resulting from devaluation of the dollar could evaporate if the United States provoked retaliatory trade actions by other nations. Even without such retaliation, there would be a lag of a year or two before the devaluation produced a strong effect on U.S. imports or exports.

The cut in consumer saving and climb in spending were postulated on the end of inflationary expectations. But the wage-price-rent freeze was the honeymoon period of the anti-inflation program. When the freeze ended, the Phase Two controls were administered rather shabbily by the Pay Board and Price Commission, which received very little prodding by the President or other high Administration officials to stiffen their resistance to inflationary wage-and-price actions. The battle against inflation was far from won.

Recent experience in the United States—and in the European democracies as well—gives reason to fear that the problem of controlling inflation is growing more intense, for three reasons:

• Unemployment is politically even more unpopular than inflation.

• Electorates have eaten of the fruit of the tree of knowledge and believe that governments and central banks can and will pump out enough money to check unemployment when it gets politically intolerable.

• People therefore expect inflation to continue (perhaps after occasional brief pauses or slowdowns), and they act accordingly. Their actions validate their expectations.

Labor unions with market power boost their wage demands to make up for past inflation and to stay ahead of future inflation, despite higher unemployment and reduced work-weeks. Business corporations with market power raise their prices to keep ahead of rising costs and to protect profit margins, despite declining sales. In fact, a relatively moderate economic slowdown may cause businesses to raise prices to protect slimming profit margins, and workers to raise pay demands to compensate for reduced work-weeks and shrunken dollars.

The inflation proved to be a tougher nut to crack than anyone expected. The monetarists—especially those within the Nixon Administration—were wrong about how long it would take to slow down the inflation and at what cost in unemployment. But the fiscalists—including those who served in the last Administration—were wrong in their forecasts, too. Neither the Nixonian nor the Kennedy-Johnsonian economists expected that so much of the impact of budgetary restraint and slower monetary growth would fall on real output and so little on prices and wages.

There is, of course, nothing wrong with the effort of a government to respond to the demand of the electorate that the unemployment problem be solved concurrently with stopping inflation. If a nation says it does not want inflation but is unwilling to stop an inflation by loading so much of the cost upon the unemployed, then it is up to politicians and their economic advisers to try to find ways of satisfying that demand.

But whether this can be done without changing fundamental national policies is another matter. How can the cost
of fighting inflation be more evenly distributed? How can
the economic behavior of pressure groups be moderated?
How can inflation be prevented from causing national and
international disorder and economic breakdowns?

These are crucial political-economic questions facing this
democracy—and many others. There has been a breakdown
of faith in both fiscalism and monetarism; simply increasing
or decreasing the total volume of dollar spending by consumers, business, government is not a sufficient answer to the
problems of either inflation or unemployment. General or
"macroeconomic" policies of stimulation or contraction need
to be reinforced by specific manpower programs and incomes
policies, if full employment is to be reconciled with price
stability. That would appear to be the cardinal economic
policy lesson of both the Johnson and Nixon years.

8. The End of Ideology?

In switching from laissez faire to controls, the Nixon Administration never conceded that it had altered its ideology. But its economists recognized that the President's freeze on prices, wages, and rents and the Phase Two controls, had raised basic questions about the future of the American economic system.

"What are we to make of these actions in the most free-market of countries by the most free-market of Presidents who, as a minor footnote, is advised by the most free-market of economists?" asked Herbert Stein. He noted two possible interpretations—that the free-price system was inadequate to the nation's present needs and would have to be radically and permanently suppressed or, on the other hand, that the free-market system possessed great virtues but was constantly on the verge of destruction by ignorant or power-hungry government officials.

"Both of these interpretations," said Mr. Stein, "are wide of the mark. The new programs were found to be required, and were imposed, in a particular historical context which is not the inherently necessary condition of free-market systems."

By the middle of the summer of 1971, it was clear that Mr. Nixon's game plan was in trouble. Inflation was once more accelerating. Unemployment was hanging around the five million level. Speculators were betting on a dollar devaluation.

In the first two weeks of August, the economic news worsened. The steel strike was settled with a contract for a 30 per cent wage increase over three years. Railroad workers won a 46 per cent wage increase over forty-two months. Wholesale prices were reported to be climbing at an annual rate of more than 8 per cent.

A congressional committee released a report stating that the dollar was overvalued and should be devalued. This gave further impetus to the outflow of dollars; foreign central banks were forced to buy up hundreds of millions of dollars to maintain the exchange rates of their currencies.

There was increasing pressure on the President to change the old game plan—and it was not only the Democrats who were howling. Secretary of the Treasury Connally, Federal Reserve Chairman Burns, and even C.E.A. Chairman McCracken were pushing for some kind of incomes policy to check the wage-price spiral. Twelve Republican senators introduced legislation to establish a wage-price board to set standards for the economy. Public-opinion polls showed strong national support for a change in economic policy.

The state of the economy was the number one issue of public concern.

A first hint of the coming change in the game plan came from the President on August 4; he indicated that his mind was open on the wage-price board question, but that he would make no move until congressional hearings could be held sometime in September. But he could not hold out that long. On the weekend of August 15, 1971, he met at Camp David with his closest economic advisers, supposedly to discuss defense spending but actually to put the final touches on what came to be called the New Economic Policy.[1] Just six weeks earlier, Secretary Connally had emerged from the first Camp David economic summit meeting to announce, as the President's newly designated "chief economic spokesman," that there would be no wage-price controls, no stabilization board, no tax cuts. Now, on a Sunday night, the President went on television to announce his own about-face. He would launch a simultaneous attack on three fronts—unemployment, inflation, and international speculation against the dollar.

Citing the winding down of the Vietnam war as a serious cause of unemployment, the President proposed a 10 per cent "job development credit"—that is, a revival of the tax credit for business investment in new plants and equipment. After one year, the 10 per cent credit would drop to 5 per cent. He also proposed to speed up personal income-tax exemptions by letting taxpayers deduct an extra $50.00 for each exemption a year earlier than planned. And, to stimu-

[1] Presidential adviser and economics speechwriter William L. Safire later said that not all members of the Quadriad—the Treasury, Office of Management and Budget, C.E.A., and Federal Reserve Board—knew the big switch in policy was coming before Camp David II actually occurred. Treasury-Secretary Connally and Budget Director Shultz certainly knew, but Arthur Burns of the F.R.B. and Paul McCracken of C.E.A. were apparently in the dark until the last minute.

late automobile-buying and production, the President asked
for repeal of the 7 per cent excise tax on cars.

To offset the loss of revenue resulting from those proposals, Mr. Nixon asked for a $4.7 billion cut in federal
spending, including a six-month postponement of pay raises
for government employees, a 5 per cent cut in government
personnel, and a 10 per cent cut in foreign economic aid.
He also asked Congress to postpone any revenue-sharing
program for three months and to put off welfare reform for
a year.

To check the inflation at once, the President announced
a freeze on all prices, wages, and rents for ninety days. Corporations were asked to extend the freeze voluntarily to
dividends. Congress had given Mr. Nixon the power to impose such a freeze—over his protests that he didn't want it—
through the Economic Stabilization Act of 1970. Although
he said the success of the freeze would depend on voluntary
compliance, the legislation provided for court injunctions
and fines as high as $5,000.

And to discourage international speculators who, said Mr.
Nixon, "thrive on crisis," he slammed the gold window shut,
declaring that the convertibility of the dollar into gold and
other reserve assets was suspended. But the President assured Americans that the dollar would be worth as much as
ever at home, and he told the nation not to fear what he
called the "bugaboo" of devaluation. To protect the dollar,
he said, he was temporarily imposing a 10 per cent surcharge
on all imports from abroad that were not already protected
by compulsory quotas. He asked Congress not to make the
"job development credit" available to American businesses
that bought capital equipment produced abroad and also
called for export subsidies for American goods. Such steps,
he said, would help end the competitive disadvantage facing

American goods in world markets owing to unfair exchange rates between foreign currencies and the dollar. When such unfair treatment of the United States ended, said the President, so would the surtax and the "buy American" clause in the investment tax credit.

The American public reaction to the President's domestic program was generally favorable, although many complained that he had waited too long. Labor criticized what it regarded as the pro-business bias of Mr. Nixon's proposed tax cuts. George Meany called the program a "tax bonanza to American corporations . . . at the expense of American workers" and "Robin Hood in reverse, because it robs from the poor and gives to the rich." Mr. Meany fumed:

> I think everything he has tried to do is a failure. He didn't give us the jobs. He didn't cool off the economy or halt inflation. He is still the handmaiden of big business as he always has been. . . . I think that he is still the same old Nixon who feels that the only way to have a prosperous America is to keep the big corporations fat and prosperous, and that all of the things he professed an interest in of a social nature he seems to be ready to let them go down the drain in order to keep big business happy.

Mr. Meany called the President's tax program "a form of socialism for big business . . . a one-sided redistribution of the public wealth."

After the initial shock of the freeze, public attention quickly turned to the most crucial part of the President's fight against inflation—what was to follow the ninety-day freeze on wages and prices. Organized labor wanted a tripartite wage-price board that would set its own rules and make decisions on a case-by-case basis without relying on the courts for enforcement. Business wanted a government board similar to the Cost of Living Council, chaired by Treasury Secretary Connally, that would lay down wage-price standards. Business preferred to accept government authority rather than accept labor participation in setting wage standards. But the Nixon Administration felt labor participation was essential to any workable program.

In his speech to a joint session of Congress on September 9, President Nixon barred an extension of the freeze but gave few hints of what was to come. An anticontrols Administration was loathe to lay down a tough program. A month later, Mr. Nixon revealed the broad design of the Phase Two apparatus but was still vague about wage-price standards. The broad objective of Phase Two, the President said, was to decrease the annual rate of price increases to 2 to 3 per cent by the end of 1972. He did not set a target for the rate of wage increase. However, a 5 to 6 per cent annual increase in wages appeared consistent with the price target of 2 to 3 per cent—assuming annual productivity gains of about 3 per cent.

The Cost of Living Council was given responsibility for coordinating wage-and-price standards and enforcement, but the President said the success of Phase Two would continue to depend on voluntary cooperation; only the largest and most important businesses would be required to report wage or price changes. Mr. Nixon delegated to a Pay Board responsibility for setting wage guidelines, examining settlements for compliance, and reviewing specific requests for adjustment. The Pay Board would be composed of fifteen members, equally divided among public, business, and labor representatives. Judge George Boldt was named chairman of the Pay Board.

A Price Commission, made up wholly of public members, was charged with setting standards and hearing appeals on prices; its chairman would be a business school dean, C. Jackson Grayson, Jr.

A Commission on Dividends and Interest Rates, to be headed by Federal Reserve Board Chairman Burns, would recommend and monitor dividend payouts and interest rates and seek voluntary restraint.

Business leaders quickly gave the President's plan their support, but labor leaders were furious over the suggestion in Mr. Nixon's speech that the Cost of Living Council would have the final word on wage-and-price changes. The labor leaders asserted that they had given prior approval to the President's plan on October 7 under the impression that the Pay Board and Price Commission would have full autonomy. George Meany said of Mr. Nixon's budget director, George P. Shultz, who handled the negotiation for the White House, "We thought we were talking to the head man, but . . . he had evidently been demoted."

Only after the labor leaders received a signed pledge from President Nixon that Pay Board decisions would not be subject to a veto by the Cost of Living Council did they agree to cooperate in Phase Two. George Meany said that labor had neither been asked to give nor had it given a no-strike pledge for Phase Two.

The stock market, which had rallied strongly immediately after the wage-price freeze was announced on August 15, began to fall apart as worries over the ineffectuality of Phase Two controls grew. The President then asked Congress to extend his authority over wages and prices under the Economic Stabilization Act of 1970 to April, 1973, and to give him the additional power to regulate interest rates and dividends. He also asked for legislation to ratify all actions previously taken under authority of the act, in order to strengthen the government's position against possible court challenges to the President's broadened powers. Congress gave the President the authority he wanted.

The new Commission on Dividends and Interest Rates was the first of the boards to act. On November 2—even before the freeze ended on November 13—the commission announced a guideline of 4 per cent for dividend increases. The base to be used in figuring the rate of increase was the total amount of dividends per share paid by a corporation in any of the fiscal years ending in 1969, 1970, or 1971. The 4 per cent standard was not expected to be applied rigidly, because Federal Reserve Board Chairman Burns had told the House Banking and Currency Committee the day before that exceptions might be made in order to help raise capital, especially in the cases of small businesses.

The interest-rate guideline of 4 per cent was undoubtedly the easiest to hold; corporations do not ordinarily long to increase their dividend payouts; all during the 1960's, a common liberal complaint was that corporations were retaining an excessive share of their earnings and using them to finance conglomerate mergers, to acquire foreign properties, to boost executive pay and perquisites, and to avoid the market test for raising additional capital.

The Nixon Administration apparently had no great desire to set a guideline for dividends but did so for two reasons: to quiet labor demands for "equity" with curbs on wages, and to set a low guideline of 4 per cent on dividends that might help to limit the standard for wages. Actually, insofar as corporate earnings grew, they tended to increase the shareholders' wealth regardless of the limit on dividends.

Setting a guideline on wages was much more troublesome. In the initial deliberations of the Pay Board, the public members initially proposed, on November 3, 1971, a 5 per cent guideline with no retroactivity during the period of the freeze. The labor members rejected this proposal.

On November 4, the labor members presented a proposal

that would have allowed wage increases consistent with productivity and cost-of-living increases, but the other members of the Pay Board objected to the vagueness of the guideline and did not accept the 6 per cent figure that labor offered the following day.

On November 5, the business members proposed a 7 per cent guideline up to January 1, 1972, and 5 per cent thereafter. But this business proposal again provided for no retroactivity and included fringe benefits in the percentage figure; once again, labor rejected it.

Then, on November 8, the Pay Board, with the labor members opposed, voted for a 5.5 per cent guideline for annual wage increases. Raises lost during the freeze would normally be barred, although the possibility remained that retroactivity might be granted in special cases, such as those in which prices had been raised in anticipation of a wage increase that had not been put into effect because of the freeze. Contracts already negotiated for the post-freeze period would be allowed to stand unless challenged by five members of the Pay Board or someone whose interests were at stake. The 5.5 per cent guideline, which included fringe benefits, was expected to be reviewed periodically and applied flexibly. Although the deferred wage increases granted by the board's decision were of greater dollar value than those lost retroactively, labor was strongly opposed to the nullification of any part of a contract and against granting to business what it saw as windfall profits from the freeze.

However, it appeared that, at least for the time being, labor members would not quit the board. Labor leaders were wary of taking actions that might destroy an effort to control inflation that had broad public support; labor leaders themselves, after all, had insisted upon the need for a national incomes policy long before Nixon was willing to adopt one.

As it turned out, it was really up to the Price Commission to restrain wage increases. On November 11, 1971, the Price Commission announced a guideline limiting price increases to an average rate of 2.5 per cent. Allowable price increases could result only from an increase in costs. Profit margins—the spread between costs and prices—were to be limited, but there would be no control on total profits; if corporations increased their total sales, their total profit would increase, even though profit margins remained the same. The base to be used in calculating acceptable price increases was the average of a company's profit margin during any two of the preceding three fiscal years. No price increases were to be granted to permit companies to make up for the period of the freeze. And companies making windfall profits as a result of the freeze were to roll back their prices.

The stock market continued to worry about the effectiveness of Phase Two controls and whether the Administration had found the right balance between firmness and flexibility. At the end of November, the Pay Board approved a 16 per cent wage increase for soft-coal miners, almost triple its own 5.5 per cent wage guideline. Secretary of Labor James D. Hodgson defended this action by the Board saying that the Administration had known all along that at the start of Phase Two it would have to "swallow" very large wage increases—not only in coal but also in such fields as aerospace, the docks, and the railroads. Indeed, in early December, the Pay Board approved that portion of the 46 per cent, forty-two-month settlement for railroad signalmen that had not already been mandated by Congress or recommended by the railroad emergency board.

The public and business members of the Pay Board were concerned over the impact of these actions on their public "credibility." But they insisted privately that they were trying to ensure against a wage explosion when Phase Two finally came to an end; this, they said, had been the fate of earlier incomes policies, here and abroad, when the lid of the pot had finally blown.

Secretary Hodgson, in keeping with this line, contended that the Pay Board's immediate job was simply to guard against a breakthrough above past wage-settlement patterns. He hoped that, when the immediate post-freeze round of wage increases was over—a round based on "parallel relationships" or "piggybacking" with other groups of workers—the Pay Board could begin to bring the wage pattern down to the guideline figure of 5.5 per cent. But one had to wait a while longer for "the last cow through the gate."

However, the Price Commission was by no means so accommodating as the Pay Board or the Administration. It refused to permit coal companies to pass through the whole of the 16 per cent labor cost increase granted to the miners and thereby squeezed company profits. Businessmen in other industries, foreseeing a precedent, worried that a disparity between Pay Board laxity and Price Commission toughness would hurt them badly and slow the business recovery.

Mr. Nixon's field general for the N.E.P. was Secretary of the Treasury John B. Connally, Jr. When Mr. Nixon picked Mr. Connally to replace David M. Kennedy, the soft-spoken Chicago banker, at the Treasury after the Republican losses in the 1970 election, the first reaction of old Washington hands was that Mr. Nixon had made a clever but politically risky move. It was clever because the President needed a Treasury Secretary with political sense, a forceful and aggressive personality, and the articulateness to do a strong selling job on a Democratically controlled Congress. Mr. Connally fit those qualifications to a T—with the extra advantage that the T stands for Texas, a state whose twenty-six electoral votes could be crucial for Mr. Nixon in 1972.

But the move was also risky because Mr. Connally, with a strong political base of his own after his three terms as Governor of Texas, would have considerable leverage on the President. If Mr. Connally, a man lacking experience in the economic and monetary areas, should blunder, the President would find it hard to control or discipline him. The political costs of firing him could be even greater for Mr. Nixon than the potential gains of having him at the Treasury.

Mr. Connally had taken the Treasury post to serve not solely the President's aims but, obviously, his own as well. As a conservative Texas political leader, closely tied to oil and gas interests, Mr. Connally did not have much hope of gaining a place on his party's ticket as presidential or vice-presidential candidate. A brilliant performance on the economic front would open up at least the second possibility for him—and perhaps eventually a shot at the top job.

In the possession of a tough and able man like Mr. Connally, the Treasury command post can be an extremely important one. Formally, the Treasury Secretary has three major jobs—adviser to the President, financial agent for the government, and law enforcement officer. But beyond this, the Treasury Secretary has a mystique and power potential fully comparable to those of the Chancellor of the Exchequer in Britain or the Minister of Finance in France. The mystique may not be all that mysterious to explain; it derives from money.

Power over money, in the hands of the right man, can enable a Secretary of the Treasury to move into every definite action of government—in military and foreign affairs, as well as in domestic economic and social affairs. In relatively recent times, the potential of the job can best be seen in the highly influential roles played by a Democrat like Henry Morgenthau under Roosevelt or a Republican like George Humphrey under Eisenhower, or, for that matter, a Republican in a Democratic Administration, like Douglas Dillon under President Kennedy (not to mention such mythical titans as Alexander Hamilton and Albert Gallatin).

Obviously, however, the power of the Secretary of the Treasury depends chiefly on his force and intelligence, and does not go, as they say in the army, with the uniform. There were several unknown factors that could have hampered Mr. Connally's effectiveness.

One question was whether he would be able to cope with what Washingtonians call the "palace guard"—the operatives in the White House who surround the President; other seemingly strong Cabinet secretaries have been shut out by the keepers of the palace doors. Mr. Connally quickly demonstrated that he would take no guff or interference from the palace guard.

A second question was whether Mr. Connally could, in fact, project a national perspective of his own and avoid being put down as a special-interest man. This could be important on matters like oil and gas depletion allowances and oil import quotas. At the Treasury, Mr. Connally walked warily on all such issues.

The third question was whether Mr. Connally—admittedly a skilled politician and advocate—had the economic understanding and sophistication to counter other policy-makers within the Administration—or at the Federal Reserve. He soon demonstrated that he was a remarkably "quick study" on economic matters—and a daring economic policy-maker.

Mr. Connally has been typecast as a conservative—and this was one reason for his being acceptable, as a Democrat, to Mr. Nixon. But those who know him best put him down, even more importantly, as a pragmatist, and Mr. Nixon could have wanted him for that reason as well—to offset the ideologues in his Administration.

Mr. Connally's first and most important job was to get the economy moving forward at a brisker rate. Two weeks before the President announced that he would name him as Secretary of the Treasury—it could well have been a reason why he was chosen—Mr. Connally made a striking speech at a meeting of the Investment Bankers Association in Boca Raton, Florida.

He told the bankers that "it is to your real interest that you spend some time helping to understand, and more than understand, helping to articulate the problems that we have in the long run of getting this nation, frankly, off its back and on its feet and back to work."

As Mr. Connally set out to do that job of reinvigorating the economy by such controversial policies as higher spending and tax cuts, he had a great potential asset through his political and personal rapport with such influential conservative or populist Democrats as Chairman Wilbur Mills (Arkansas) of the House Ways and Means Committee, Chairman George Mahon (Texas) of the House Appropriations Committee, and Chairman Wright Patman (Texas) of the House Banking and Currency Committee.

But Mr. Connally proved to be valuable to the President not only in selling his fiscal policies to Congress but in economic policy battles within the Administration. Although Mr. Nixon had cautiously begun to enunciate an "incomes policy" by the end of 1970 and to call for "special restraint" from business and labor, in response to pressures from

Chairman Burns of the Federal Reserve Board, there was heavy resistance from within Mr. Nixon's own fold—perhaps most importantly from George P. Shultz, the Director of the Office of Management and Budget—to wage-price restraints and guidelines.

In his Boca Raton speech, Mr. Connally declared, "With the weapons that they [the Nixon Administration] have, I do not think they can wholly accomplish their purpose short of wage-and-price controls, something which they don't want to ask for and which the American people don't want imposed."

Mr. Connally's fellow Texan, Under Secretary of the Treasury Charls E. Walker, a Republican, from the beginning said he expected the former Texas governor to be "wholly pragmatic" about measures for breaking the wage-price spiral, and "not wed to any theories like the ideological types in this Administration." If Mr. Connally were able to wage a more effective campaign against economic stagnation and unemployment, on one side, and against inflation, on the other, than Mr. Nixon's Friedmanesque economic generals had conducted, he would not only advance the President's political ambitions but do wonders for his own.

But to complete the three-way economic hat trick, Mr. Connally would also have to win in the international area—and there he faced even stiffer opposition from foreign governments than he did from the Democrats in Congress or the so-called ideologues in the Nixon Administration. The roots of the conflicts between the United States and its major trading partners were deep and tangled.

9. On the Brink

Unpacking his bags, an American back from Europe
in the late fall of 1970 found some curious souvenirs. *Item*:
Glass from a shattered car window, hit by a rock hurled in
Copenhagen by a student demonstrating against World
Bank President Robert McNamara, former U.S. Secretary
of Defense. *Item*: Swedish politician talking—"Vietnam was
not an issue in our election campaign. Nobody would defend
U.S. policy." *Item*: American banker based in Europe—"I
have never heard so much pessimism and unease expressed
about the United States." *Item*: Sign in window of Swiss
hair-dressing shop—"Our wigs made from Swiss hair."

Europe was booming. To one who remembered it from
the period immediately after World War II, the contrast
was staggering. From an old notebook of 1946: *Item:* "Daily

caloric intake—Paris, 1,900; Rome, 1,600; Brussels, 1,950; Berlin, 1,275 (U.S. Zone)." *Item*: "Black-market operation in men's room at Hotel Metropole in francs, pounds, dollars, crowns, marks." *Item*: "Truck broke down in street, full of German PW's. Belgians swarmed around, trying to get at them, screaming 'Schweinhund!' MP's pushed them back." *Item*: American surgeon general in Berlin—"There's a psychological factor—no will to live. We're facing a debasement of the people. If you fed them, it would be a different story."

Almost twenty-five years later, Europe was fat and sassy and quite willing to lecture to the United States on its economic deficiencies. European economic growth rates had been stronger and steadier than America's. Its share of international trade was much larger and growing faster.

The postwar dollar gap was a dim memory. Europeans were holding more dollars than they wanted, and they complained that the United States would not give them gold, or at least Special Drawing Rights (S.D.R.'s). Europe felt financially stronger than the United States. European monetary reserves—including gold, dollars, S.D.R.'s, and drawing rights at the International Monetary Fund (I.M.F.) —exceeded $31 billion, while U.S. monetary reserves amounted to only $16 billion. And European reserves were still growing fast, while American reserves were shrinking.

Yet such numbers only measured the frustration of the Europeans. Despite their growing economic weight, the separate small and medium-sized nations of Europe still felt incapable of coping with the massed and concentrated resources of America. The determination to hold off the American giant was the basic motivation behind the current European drive to turn the Common Market into an economic and monetary union. The Europeans were convinced that the U.S. industrial and financial penetration of their territory had been greatly facilitated by the role of the dollar as a reserve currency and the vast growth of the Eurodollar market.

So, at the Brussels headquarters of the Common Market, a push was on to take the first step toward a common European currency. That first step would involve a closer tying together of their currencies, with only a 0.75 per cent fluctuation above or below par values.

The exercise of forcing their currencies together, the financial leaders of Europe believed, would force their central banks to work closely together. In due course this would mean, they argued, a development of supranational economic institutions, including a Federal Reserve Bank for Europe, with a European reserve money that would cut Europe loose from dependency on the dollar.

But, both within and outside the Common Market's top political and financial circles, there remained great skepticism that this device of using a common money as the instrument for building a new united Europe would work. The skeptics contended that monetary union could come only after economic and political integration, not before. And some insisted that a true European state was not one decade but many decades away; immediately, they said, European nationalists were simply trying to rid themselves of American dominance.

Yet European attitudes toward America were a complicated mixture of aggression and dependence. This was even true in the economic area, where European governments frequently sought to attract investment, and European firms still wanted access to American technology as well as financial resources.

But it remained particularly true in the military area,

where Europe was far from prepared to take on the responsibility for its own defense. The European defense ministers, meeting at North Atlantic Treaty Organization (NATO) headquarters in Brussels, had in 1970 committed their countries to the principle of assuming a greater share of the burdens carried by the United States in Europe. This decision represented a belated recognition of the strong currents running in the U.S. Congress—and presumably among the American people—for military cutbacks not only in Southeast Asia but all over the world. But top NATO officers argued that U.S. forces in Europe had already taken heavy cuts. All three military forces in the European command were at lower levels than at any time in the preceding dozen years. NATO officers worried that the support for combat forces for a meaningful nonnuclear defense of Europe had been hollowed out to the danger point. They maintained that the over-all balance between Warsaw Pact conventional forces and NATO conventional forces in central Europe was shifting in favor of the Communist bloc.

Although concerned about strains on the U.S. budget —and piqued by European criticism of American balance-of-payments deficits—American officials contended that the actual dollars savings from transferring U.S. forces from Europe to the continental United States would be negligible. West German offset agreements, they said, covered 80 per cent of U.S. balance-of-payments costs.

But the main concern of NATO heads was strategic, not economic. They feared that if heavy unilateral cuts were imposed on U.S. conventional forces, this would lower the nuclear threshold and accelerate the time when tactical nuclear weapons might have to be used to defend American and West European troops in the event of a Russian miscalculation.

There is another reason, they insisted, why the United States should exercise caution in pulling troops out of Europe—the evolving strength of West Germany in Europe. One important purpose for stationing U.S. troops in Europe was to provide reassurance behind which the Germans could develop economic and financial strength without fear of a backlash from their West European neighbors or from the Soviets. This reason should not be forgotten, especially now that the Germans may be emerging as a more autonomous power in world politics, in the wake of the German–Soviet treaty for normalizing relations and the pending German–Soviet trade agreement, which may have a highly significant bearing on the degree of commitment of Germany to the Common Market. Thus, the European scene—which on the surface looked like a fairly simple case of a rebuilt Europe striking out for its own identity and independence from America—was turning out to be a much trickier and deeper story. On the one side, the Europeans were indulging themselves in a mood of anti-Americanism. They saw America's economic problems, social disorder, and military failure in Vietnam as evidence of this country's declining power.

But the Europeans still knew that they needed America militarily as well as economically. For there was a long way to go before Europe could unite politically and economically, build a strong defense of its own, or play a significant foreign-policy role outside Europe—for instance, in Asia or the Middle East. Thus, the dominant European mood was one of frustration, and the opportunity for getting richer was providing the main outlet for national energies.

"Confidence is suspicion asleep," said Benjamin Disraeli. After a remarkably quiet year in the international money markets, suspicion about the dollar had reawakened. The

United States ran a deficit of more than $10 billion in 1970. When you asked an American monetary official what would happen if this deficit rate were to continue for a year, the answer you got was, "Nothing." Those who answered so contended that the world had been on a dollar standard since March, 1968, when the major financial powers stopped pegging the price of gold in the private market; the Americans contended that foreigners would not refuse to go on accepting dollars in settlement of U.S. deficits—because, if they did, the world's monetary system would collapse. However, if the Europeans wanted to let the value of their currencies appreciate in relation to the dollar, that was perfectly all right with the Americans, since it would improve the U.S. balance of payments. Either way, the United States was sitting pretty, and there was no point in paying much attention to its balance-of-payments deficits. This was the era of "benign neglect," a term that American officials publicly deplored and privately accepted and used.

But many Europeans thought the Americans were living in a dream world. One high French official, asked what he really thought would happen if the huge dollar outflow continued, shrugged and exploded, "Something!"

Raymond Barre, a vice president of the European Economic Community (E.E.C.), said, "No one wants a crisis for the dollar, which would be a crisis for the entire international monetary system, but, under the pressure of violations of the fundamental rules of the system, the moment will come when it will no longer be possible to keep control over events."

Efforts to resolve the money muddle were going nowhere. American officials said that foreign currencies—especially the Japanese yen and the Deutsche mark—were undervalued and should be raised. The foreigners said the deficit was

America's, and the Americans should get it under control. But they were divided on what the United States should do. Some of the economists said, "Devalue the dollar." The Americans replied that this was impossible—other currencies were pegged to the dollar and would come down with it. Though the economists said this was not necessarily so, many European business interests were opposed to the trading advantage that a dollar devaluation would give the United States—the same reason they opposed a European upvaluation of currencies.

Old-fashioned Europeans still felt that a paper standard would breed endless inflation. But even Jacques Rueff, once Charles de Gaulle's chief financial adviser, had concluded that it was too late for a return to what the general had called "the immutability, the impartiality, the universality, which are the privileges of gold." The Americans rudely said, "Gold is dead." They offered the world the choice between dollars and Special Drawing Rights, the created monetary reserves of the International Monetary Fund, more simply known as "paper gold."

The "good Europeans"—champions of full political and economic union—hoped to create a new European money, but few expected that this could be achieved in the ten-year period sketched in Brussels, and some thought it would never happen. The idealists dreamed of a world money; William McChesney Martin was calling for a World Federal Reserve Bank.

But while the long money debate went on, a solution that nobody would say he wanted was emerging. That solution was a retreat from liberal trade and freely flowing investments back to protectionism and national self-sufficiency.

In a sense, the protectionist virus is always present in the blood stream of every nation's industry. It takes only a spell of monetary disorder and the inability to cope with foreign competition because of an overvalued currency to activate the virus and produce a protectionist epidemic. What starts with textiles can spread to shoes, steel, electronics, autos, anything. What starts in one country—such as the United States—can spread to many others.

European liberals were dismayed over President Nixon's ambivalent trade policy. "The United States has no trade policy," they said. They were astonished at the lengths to which the President was willing to go to deliver on a political commitment to restrict Japanese textile shipments —even to the point of threatening to block the agreement to restore Okinawa to Japan.

But they recognized that the Americans had been provoked, both by the Europeans and by Japan. The Common Market remains highly protectionist on agricultural products. Still heard in Europe is one of General de Gaulle's maxims: "One eats what one produces, not what one imports." Whatever it may lack in French logic, this pronouncement has the mystical quality that appeals to French farmers —and many others. Similarly, Japan has been far too slow in liberalizing trade and foreign investment and has moved only under extreme threats. The Europeans are now afraid that if the Americans exclude Japanese textiles or other goods, they will be inundated—and have to boost their trade walls against industrial goods.

Europeans don't want a trade war. "You don't want a war when you are building a cathedral," they say. Some would like America instead to cut back its capital exports to Europe. One French official had proposed that the United States adopt multiple exchange rates, with penalty rates on capital investment in Europe. The ghost of Hjalmar Schacht was still around. A return to protectionism, capital controls, Schachtian exchange rates and all that would be a tragedy for the industrial nations of the West, both economically and politically.

There was no sign that the Nixon Administration was prepared to provide the leadership to reverse the trend toward protectionism. And there was no reason to expect that the Common Market could do the job. Japan, insecure and inexperienced, could not lead. Who could? International civil servants? Some would certainly try. But the truth was that, to get out of the box, the United States, Europe, and Japan would all have to move. If the political will were lacking to make a concerted effort in the international arena, "something," as the Frenchman said, was bound to happen.

10. R. I. P. Bretton Woods

So the major financial powers of the world were on the verge of their most serious monetary crisis since World War II, but almost nobody knew what was going on. To the uninitiated, nothing can be more esoteric than a meeting of the International Monetary Fund, such as the one that took place in September, 1970, in Copenhagen, city of schnapps, fairy tales, and pornography. Among the masses of paper gushing forth from the mimeograph machines for the delectation of finance ministers and central bankers there was, unfortunately, no glossary of terms. This was a considerable handicap not only for newspaper reporters, left-wing demonstrators, and wives and children of delegates but even for quite a few delegates themselves.

In a desperate and certainly futile effort to repair this

lack, the following glossary was prepared at the last minute:

Par Values of Currencies: Every nation wanting to join the International Monetary Fund must, first of all, have some money. Once each country has satisfied this condition (as 116 now have), it must pick a par value for its money.

For instance, Afghanistan has a currency called afghani; one afghani is officially equal to .00197482 grams of pure gold per unit. There are 1,575 afghani per troy ounce of gold. One afghani also equals 2.22222 (it stops there) U.S. cents and forty-five afghani equal one dollar.

If countries don't like their old par values, they are supposed to talk to the International Monetary Fund about it before they make a change in excess of 10 per cent of the initial parity.

If they do not talk to the Fund, the Fund's feelings are hurt, and it grumbles. Canada has recently hurt the Fund's feelings by allowing its currency to float without talking to the Fund, and it floated up from being worth 92.5 U.S. cents (give or take 1 per cent) to being worth about 98-¾ cents when last seen.

West Germany also floated the mark for a while last fall, but that was tolerated because West Germany was nice about it and didn't do it too long.

Floating Exchange Rate System: Some economists think it would be great if all currencies floated up and down indefinitely like the Canadian dollar.

The executive directors of the International Monetary Fund think this is a horrible idea and have just banned it from any further discussion. The economists will not pay any attention to them.

Those economists who like floating exchange rates say that these will automatically keep currencies at their correct values in relation to each other. But the I.M.F. Directors say it will breed all kinds of instability and misery, and that nobody will ever know what his money is going to be worth. This, they claim, will damage trade and investment.

But floating-rate economists say this is nonsense, and that floating rates will remove obstacles from trade and investment. There is no end to this controversy.

Fundamental Disequilibrium: The I.M.F. is not absolutely against exchange-rate changes when a nation's currency is in fundamental disequilibrium. Unfortunately, nobody knows what fundamental disequilibrium is.

A deliberate decision was made at Bretton Woods, New Hampshire, in 1944 not to define fundamental disequilibrium, because once you did, countries might change the value of their currency too often or not often enough.

Pierre-Paul Schweitzer, Managing Director of the I.M.F., has now hinted at a definition of fundamental disequilibrium by saying that the Fund's directors have now reaffirmed the "real Bretton Woods philosophy."

This means, he says, that "if you try to restore equilibrium only by domestic measures, it might be sometimes impossible or you would have to have recourse to such drastic measures that it would seriously affect domestic prosperity."

He also suggests that fundamental disequilibrium exists when, if you don't change your exchange rate, you are likely to have to restrict your trade and payments with other countries. This could mean the United States, except that nobody thinks the United States can devalue.

Wider Bands: The I.M.F. will also probably decide to study the question of whether currencies can float a little bit more than they do within the 1 per cent margin around their par value.

Some Fund directors think it might be all right to think about studying 2 per cent or maybe even 3 per cent bands.

Other directors think this would not be a good thing to study.

But all the directors agree that it would not be a good idea to study any wider bands than 3 per cent.

The directors seem agreed that if a study showed that it were a good idea to make the bands a little wider, this would require amending the Bretton Woods articles of agreement.

But they also agree that if some countries want to live within narrower bands than 1 per cent, that is all right.

This is a very important point for countries within the Common Market that are now trying to tie their currencies closer and closer together and finally meld them into one.

Some of the countries appear to regard the effort to widen bands, which the U.S. Treasury seems to favor, as a nasty American plot to prevent full integration of the Common Market.

The United States Treasury says this is a big fib.

Rate Flexibility: Some countries also say that the United States wants exchange-rate flexibility for other countries, so that they will move their currencies upward in value and make it unnecessary for the United States to straighten out its economic problems, especially its inflation and the deficits in its balance of payments with others.

The Europeans argue that the United States is choking them with excess dollars. Some say they are nervous about the dollar.

Mr. Schweitzer himself says the United States should stop forcing all those dollars on other people.

Until it cuts the size of its deficits, he says, the United States should at least shell out reserves—gold and Special Drawing Rights—rather than dollars.

Otherwise, he thinks, the I.M.F. will lose control over the

growth of total reserves, which includes American dollars held by foreigners as well as gold and S.D.R.'s, and this will worsen world inflation.

Special Drawing Rights: They are vulgarly called "paper gold." They could just about as legitimately be called "paper dollars."

The issuance of $9.5 billion worth of S.D.R.'s was authorized in September, 1969, and the first batch of $3.5 billion was put out to 104 countries January 1, 1971. The United States now holds about $961 million worth of S.D.R.'s.

There appears to be a general feeling among other countries that the United States should cough up some of those S.D.R.'s to settle its debts to others.

Incomes Policy: The I.M.F. says the United States would not cause so much trouble for others if it would do a better job of controlling inflation by installing an incomes policy.

There are all sorts of incomes policies, ranging from dirty looks by presidents or prime ministers at wage or price decisions that they don't like, to wage-price-profit-dividend-interest-rent controls.

The I.M.F. does not say exactly what kind of incomes policy it recommends. The Nixon Administration does not particularly like this friendly but vague advice. In fact, it hates it.

Crawling Pegs: These are used in backgammon. Otherwise, you can forget them, because the I.M.F. has ruled them out forever.

Forever was a short time. Less than one year later, President Nixon suspended convertibility between the dollar and gold on August 15, 1971, and an obituary notice was circulated at the International Monetary Fund in Washington. It read:

R.I.P. We regretfully announce the not unexpected passing away after a long illness of Bretton Woods, at 9 P.M. last Sunday. Bretton was born in New Hampshire in 1944, and died a few days after his 27th birthday. Although abandoned by some of his parents in infancy, he was a sturdy lad and was expected to survive. Alas, in the early nineteen-sixties liquidity anaemia set in. . . .

The fatal stroke occurred this month when parasites called speculators inflated his most important member, and caused a rupture of his vital element, dollar-gold convertibility.

Memorial services will be held in Washington, D.C., on Sept. 27 at the Sheraton Park Hotel. In lieu of gold, the family will accept donations in foreign exchange to support the foundation created by Mr. Woods. No decisions have been taken as to how to allocate these donations among the potential legatees.

But what monetary system will replace Bretton Woods?

The Nixon Administration might be happiest to keep the world on the dollar standard that has essentially prevailed since free dollar-gold convertibility began to disappear in the early 1960's, when the Kennedy Administration began leaning on other governments not to claim gold but to take various types of American I O U's instead—including more dollars than they wanted to hold.

What made the foreigners so unhappy was the special privilege the United States enjoyed because the dollar was used as a monetary reserve. This meant that the United States could settle its payments deficits with other countries by printing dollars without limit.

Foreigners insisted that, without their having any control over U.S. foreign policy, they were forced to finance American military adventures abroad, such as the Vietnam war, of which they disapproved. And they contended that the huge flow of dollars overseas enabled American corporations to buy up foreign businesses, in effect paying for them out of the deficits in the U.S. balance of payments.

The Nixon Administration was originally rather indifferent to those payments deficits. The policy of benign neglect implied that the United States should focus its economic policy on domestic objectives, permitting the balance of payments to develop as it would. If, given U.S. deficits, foreigners preferred not to hold so many dollars, the Administration felt that they should upvalue their currencies to make their goods more expensive and American goods cheaper, and thereby cure the deficit and receive fewer dollars.

The worsening international crisis over the dollar ended this policy. Mr. Nixon's New Economic Policy represented a sharp turn away from benign neglect in the international area. It added a much more aggressive assault on the trade front, with threats to limit foreign access to the U.S. market if other countries did not reduce artificial barriers to U.S. exports. The Administration also demanded that foreigners increase their share of mutual defense burdens.

The key aim of the new policy was a surplus in the U.S. balance of payments, as Secretary of the Treasury John B. Connally stressed at the London meeting of the Group of Ten in September, 1971. The Administration felt that, with a balance-of-payments surplus, the United States would regain its international economic strength, which it regarded as critical to its international political power. Dollars would still be held by other countries as monetary reserves. The dollar would serve as the so-called *numéraire,* or common denominator, for all other currency values. Mr. Connally said he saw no need for the United States to change the fixed ratio between the dollar and gold at $35.00 an ounce. The Administration was in no hurry, and did not desire, to go back to buying and selling gold.

Further, the Administration believed, a strong dollar

would provide the basis for a continued system of relatively fixed exchange rates, although Washington did want somewhat wider bands of fluctuation around existing parities and greater flexibility for other currencies—and it particularly wanted those currencies that it regarded as undervalued to move up in relation to the dollar.

Thus, if the original Administration line prevailed, the world would stay on a modified dollar-standard. The growth in world monetary reserves would come not from gold nor mainly from continuous deficits in the U.S. balance of payments, as had been the case during the past two decades, but from increases in created monetary reserves—Special Drawing Rights.

Foreign governments were sharply opposed to a resolution of the present crisis that would leave the dollar with all of its old privileges. This appeared to be why the European countries, with the backing of Britain and Japan, insisted that the United States devalue the dollar in terms of gold as part of an over-all settlement. In London, at the Group of Ten meeting, the I.M.F.'s Pierre-Paul Schweitzer offered what he described as a compromise solution between the American and European positions, calling for:

• A general realignment of exchange rates of the world's leading currencies, including an upward revaluation of the major European currencies and the Japanese yen, and the devaluation of the U.S. dollar.

• A new reserve system, in which Special Drawing Rights in the I.M.F. would assume some of the reserve role of backing currencies now held by gold.

• An effort to swing the United States balance of payments from its current deficit to a surplus, with America's allies assuming a share of the burden.

• After the achievement of these steps, removal of the 10 per cent surcharge on U.S. imports.

West German Economics Minister Karl Schiller welcomed the Schweitzer proposal as a good one, but the Nixon Administration remained strongly opposed to devaluing the dollar in terms of gold. Former member of President Nixon's Council of Economic Advisers Hendrik Houthakker, now back at his professorship at Harvard, suggested that one major reason the Administration was refusing to consider a dollar evaluation in gold was that this would present it with a grueling battle in Congress. Professor Houthakker cautioned foreigners that Congress would very likely use such a request as the occasion for a wild outburst of protectionist legislation and warned them against opening this Pandora's box. Until the United States got the currency realignment it wanted from other countries, the Administration hinted, it was prepared to let the dollar float indefinitely. Mr. Nixon also threatened to hold on to the 10 per cent import surcharge to induce foreign governments to come to terms with the United States not only on exchange rates but on barriers to U.S. exports, on providing freer access to U.S. capital, particularly in Japan, and on defense burden-sharing.

Some American economists, including such otherwise conflicting thinkers as Yale's James Tobin and Chicago's Milton Friedman, would have been glad to see the dollar float indefinitely. They believed that a floating system would be the optimal monetary system to replace Bretton Woods. But they were opposed to the Administration's combination of a floating dollar with the retention of protectionist economic devices.

However, despite a widespread preference among economists for floating rates—or at least a much more flexible rate system than now exists—many economists believe that the time has not yet come when most nations are ready to move to a floating system.

Economic skeptics feel that, so long as export industries can be hurt by changes in exchange rates governed by the market, governments subject to political pressures will not let currencies float freely but will continuously intervene in foreign-exchange markets, thereby preventing international equilibrium from developing.

Since the world does not yet appear ready for a true floating-rate system, the search is on for some other monetary system to replace both Bretton Woods and the dollar standard. Despite American preferences for the dollar standard, many economists believe that foreign resistance now is too serious for the United States to take that course. Indeed, some economists believe that it would not even be in the American interest—and they would much prefer to have the dollar gain flexibility comparable to that of any other currency.

The two key reforms that appear crucial to a new monetary system, in the judgment of some leading U.S. economists, are:

• Substituting Special Drawing Rights for dollars as the common standard of value of the monetary system—that is, specifying all par values for currencies, including the U.S. dollar, in terms of S.D.R.'s.
• Gradually replacing gold, dollars, and other national currencies in official reserves with S.D.R.'s.

The time has come for a basic reconstruction of an international monetary system that has bred crisis after crisis through most of the past decade—and that had finally caused the breakdown of the Bretton Woods system.

In September, 1959, a group of the world's leading economists gathered at Elsinore, Denmark—the scene of Hamlet's tragic story—to enjoy the autumn weather by the sea and to condemn inflation. But on the first day of their meeting, Professor Robert Triffin of Yale arose like Hamlet's father's ghost to warn the economists of a greater danger than inflation. The international monetary system, he said, could not go on expanding indefinitely, based as it was on gold and national currencies, especially the dollar.

A day would come, Professor Triffin predicted, when the monetary system would fall apart as it had done in 1931, dragging the world into deep depression, unless a new international money were created to supplant dollars and gold.

In September, 1971, at the International Monetary Fund's meetings in Washington, Professor Triffin had the pleasure, granted to very few Cassandras, of hearing the finance ministers of the major nations repeating his grim prophecy and calling for his own remedy as though they were listening to a voice in the air. However, the more sophisticated ministers knew that the voice they heard was that of Professor Triffin. He had foreseen back in 1959 two evolving threats to the international monetary system.

The first derived from the difficulty of providing enough gold for an expanding world economy. Gold production and Soviet gold sales were not keeping pace with the increase of world trade or with the need of nations to increase their monetary reserves to cover their balance-of-payments deficits.

The second threat resulted from the first. To palliate the gold shortage, the capitalist nations were rebuilding the old gold-exchange system. Increasingly, they were using U.S. dollars as monetary reserves, acquired through the deficits in the American balance of payments. But Professor Triffin warned that chronic U.S. deficits would inevitably undermine confidence in the dollar. A dollar crisis would come when nations had acquired more dollars than they were willing to hold. During the 1960's, the crisis was forestalled when the United States induced other nations to convert dollars into other forms of debt. The master of this Fabian defense of the dollar was Under Secretary of the Treasury Robert V. Roosa. But that defense could not last indefinitely. The first massive attack on the dollar standard came in March, 1968. It was staved off by the creation of the two-tier gold system, which prevented private holders of dollars from claiming official gold.

The second blow to the dollar came in May, 1971. It was brought on by the rush of hot money out of dollars and into German marks and other European currencies, partly as a result of interest-rate differentials between the United States and Europe, partly because of rumors of an impending German upvaluation, but most fundamentally because of the widespread belief that the dollar had been weakened by a long series of American deficits in the balance of payments.

American government officials went on insisting that the dollar was as strong as ever. Indeed, they had taken this line throughout the preceding decade. American administrations have always been convinced that when they really wanted to, they could eliminate the deficit in the balance of payments. At the end of the 1950's, the Eisenhower Administration urged European nations to pick up more of the West's defense burdens, step up their own foreign aid and capital exports, and drop discrimination against dollar goods. Nevertheless, the payments gap was not closed. Vietnam and a step-up in U.S. inflation widened the gap after the mid-1960's.

However, Professor Triffin had foreseen that the real trouble would begin not while the balance-of-payments deficits of the United States continued but when they were ended. The reason was that "a successful readjustment of the United States balance of payments is bound to bring to the fore the latent crisis of international liquidity."

As the liquidity squeeze developed, the high pace of expansion in the world economy maintained since the end of World War II would slow down. Nations would feel increasing pressures to clamp on trade-and-exchange restrictions or to engage in competitive devaluations. These pressures would spread from country to country and might be aggravated by speculative capital movements "culminating in a financial panic à la 1931," said Professor Triffin.

The decision of President Nixon on August 15, 1971, to suspend gold convertibility and float the dollar, together with his imposition of the 10 per cent imports surcharge, were intended to close the U.S. balance-of-payments gap and swing it into surplus.

The world now faces the necessity of finding a new source of liquidity other than dollars or gold. Special Drawing Rights, created as a supplement to gold and dollars as monetary reserves only in 1970, may ultimately replace them. Some economists would prefer a system of floating exchange rates that would keep nations' payments in continuous balance, thereby obviating the need for monetary reserves to cover deficits.

But most proposals for international monetary reform being offered these days are a blend of these two key elements—new international monetary reserves and more flexible exchange rates.

Which route or combination of routes the world takes toward reform is a matter of politics more than economics. Nations highly sensitive to the pressures of industrial interest groups at home will not let the international markets freely determine exchange rates. Similarly, nations anxious to bind their economies closer together—such as the European Common Market countries—want highly stable exchange rates but realize this means they must closely coordinate their monetary and fiscal policies.

The major monetary powers—the United States, West Germany, France, Britain, and Japan—are not yet ready to choose either the course of closer integration or floating exchange rates. "These two roads are very different and it is extremely difficult to determine in which direction the international monetary system will evolve," says Lawrence B. Krause of the Brookings Institution. "At this juncture, however, the world can keep one foot on each path without much discomfort," he believes.

Whether the world can actually straddle the two routes of greater flexibility of exchange rates and closer economic integration, or whether it must choose one route or the other is the crucial issue for world monetary reform.

However, to reject both of those routes would mean the fracturing of the international monetary system and a growing trend toward protectionism, capital controls, and economic self-sufficiency for individual nations and regional blocs.

When Mr. Nixon formally suspended the dollar's convertibility on August 15, 1971, the United States still owned more than $10 billion worth of gold. But foreign official holdings of dollars exceeded $40 billion, and private dollar-holdings totaled more than $30 billion. While only official dollar-holders could ask Uncle Sam to hand over gold from Fort Knox, some part of the private dollar-holdings could have been shifted to governments as claims against American treasure.

For many years, some monetary sophisticates had scoffed at the notion that foreign governments could or would drive the United States off gold. Like a private bank, they said, the United States did not need 100 per cent reserves. Further, they contended, the dollar was "as good as gold"—not only because it represented a claim against American goods but also because foreign governments would not want to see their own currencies increase in value relative to the dollar. To let the dollar depreciate in value would be to make American goods cheaper and their own more expensive. From an American standpoint, however, that would be just fine.

Years of deficits had turned the dollar into an overvalued currency, with harmful effects on the American economy. Here is how the mechanism worked: U.S. payments deficits had put more dollars into the hands of foreigners than they really wanted to hold. Had they simply unloaded their surplus dollars in a free market, the value of the dollar would have dropped.

But under the rules of the International Monetary Fund, nations were required to maintain the price of their currencies within 1 per cent of their official parity with the dollar. As a result of the overvaluation of the dollar, American export industries and import-competing industries increasingly lost ground in foreign markets. In addition, American capital rushed abroad—not only to utilize foreign labor and materials but also to buy up foreign business at what amounted to foreign-government-subsidized prices. The U.S. trade position worsened. A drop in U.S. interest rates aggravated the outflow of funds early in 1971. Dollar balances in the hands of foreigners mounted at an alarming rate. Foreigners were fearful of being left holding the bag.

Since convertibility between the dollar and gold was suspended by President Nixon, foreign governments have come to want a new monetary system. They now insist on the end of the old dollar standard, which gave the United States unlimited credit-card facilities. They assert that it used these free borrowing privileges not only to buy up their own industries but to finance the war in Vietnam. This is why many foreign governments, including even the French, have finally been converted to the idea of a system based on a truly international reserve asset, created out of thin air, and similar to Special Drawing Rights.

S.D.R.'s may not be the precise name for the new medium, since they were originally intended to be, in part, repayable loans to nations from the I.M.F. rather than a pure monetary reserve. Perhaps S.D.R.'s might be renamed Internationals, General Reserves, Triffins, Keynesians, or—the name that John Maynard Keynes originally wanted for international money—Bancors.

But what is to be done with the gold and dollars that nations are currently holding, if the world is to shift to a new international money? Professor Triffin, Dr. Edward M. Bernstein, and other economists have various schemes for coaxing countries to turn their gold, dollars, sterling, Swiss francs, or other foreign currencies held as reserves over to the I.M.F. as a credit for the new money.

One favorite scheme for inducing nations to give up gold, which is noninterest-bearing, is to pay interest on the new reserve medium. The I.M.F. might earn the interest to be paid on the new reserves by converting all national currencies into a permanent earnings base for the Fund by the issuance of securities. The I.M.F. would thus become a true central bank for central banks.

C. Fred Bergsten, who has served as White House international monetary adviser, proposes that foreign governments exchange the billions of dollars they are holding for S.D.R.'s; these dollars would then be returned to the United States and used to retire an equivalent amount of the national debt. The dollars would thus be "monetized"—that is, turned into international money—rather than funded as debts of the United States to other nations. In effect, nations holding dollars would, according to the Bergsten plan, be asked to make a partial repayment of U.S. Marshall Plan grants and other military expenditures. This would lift a repayment obligation from the United States that its grants to other nations had helped to cause.

Mr. Bergsten maintains that this reverse Marshall Plan would not have any real cost to the foreign countries, who would simply be exchanging one reserve asset for another. But Mr. Bergsten thinks such an act could play an important role in improving U.S.- European and -Japanese relations, since it would probably be taken by Congress and the American people as an act of good will toward the United States. He thinks it would, at the same time, help to make the shift away from the dollar standard more acceptable to the United States. This country would probably choose to continue taking its chances with the outstanding dollar balances rather than accept a fixed schedule for paying them off. The United States has already demonstrated that it is willing to declare complete inconvertibility—since it feels that it has the economic strength as a market for foreign goods and as a supplier of capital to other countries to protect itself against any nation seeking to punish it for not redeeming its dollar debts.

The great advantage for the United States of shifting from a dollar standard to an S.D.R. standard is that the American currency would then be able to fluctuate in relation to S.D.R.'s just as any foreign currency does. This would give the United States an instrument for correcting imbalances in its own balance of payments without resorting to protectionist trade measures or capital controls, and without imposing the whole burden of exchange-rate adjustment on other countries. However, shifting off the dollar standard would also mean that the United States would have to accept the same international discipline on its ability to finance its deficits as other countries.

Critics contend that this would mean a loss of U.S. economic sovereignty, power, and freedom of action. But proponents say it would represent a wise departure from the self-destructive effort to maintain dollar hegemony over the non-Communist world. Sharing international responsibilities more equally could improve political and economic relations among the United States, Europe, and Japan, which are now in danger of serious deterioration.

11. Meanwhile, Back at the Common Market

A student once demanded of Professor Morris Raphael Cohen, the renowned philosopher of the City College of New York, "Can you prove that I exist?" "Even if I could prove it," said Professor Cohen, "to whom would I address my reply?" In searching for help on the dollar crisis, Secretary of the Treasury John B. Connally said that he had been addressing urgent messages to the European Economic Community but not getting an answer. Yet, in Brussels, officials insisted that Europe existed and indeed had been strengthened by the American moves.

Viscount d'Avignon, Director General of the Belgian Ministry of Foreign Affairs, conceded that the Nixon-Connally bombshells of August 15, 1971, "hit us when we were apart, drove us farther apart, but will bring us together."

He maintained that effective multilateral actions always required two conditions—first, that they be workable, and second, that nations be forced to act together by some great danger, as the Soviet thrust into Europe forced NATO to form. D'Avignon thought that the U.S. decision to float the dollar and press the Europeans to upvalue their currency and grant trade concessions was forcing Europe to speed up its plans for full monetary and economic union.

Nevertheless, in mid-November, 1971, the Germans, with the mark still floating, and the French, determined to give the dollar no trading advantage and to take whatever advantage they could of the upvaluation of other currencies, were split.

In Brussels, many observers were skeptical about European monetary integration. Cecil de Strijcker, Vice Governor of the National Bank of Belgium, said, "No other money is ready to take over the role of the dollar."

In Antwerp, President Maurice Naessens of the Banque de Paris et Des Pays Bas—had said that the dollar was strengthening. With the franc still pegged to the dollar, in effect, and with European businessmen increasingly gloomy about the prospect of a European recession, Naessens thought the dollar had already reached the limit of its relative devaluation and was more likely to move the other way.

This did not make bankers in Antwerp unhappy. Antwerp had flourished on foreign trade and investment, and thought very well of American dollars.

Flying around the sprawling port of Antwerp, you pass over the new plants of Union Carbide, Monsanto, General Motors, Ford, Chevron, Esso, Occidental Petroleum, and many other multinational companies. These tangible manifestations of the dollar invasion of Europe—and of the Eurodollar market that U.S. payments deficits helped to create—

are more impressive to Antwerp's bankers and businessmen than the ideological designs of Brussels. It is not that Antwerp does not appreciate the contribution of the Common Market to its prosperity. It knows full well that its growth as a port has depended heavily not only on American dollar flows and other foreign investment but also on the growth of the hinterland.

However, the Six exchange goods among themselves by rail, road, river, and canal. Antwerp—a booming competitor of Rotterdam, Le Havre, and Hamburg—loads the products of Europe for overseas shipments and receives huge cargoes from abroad. It looks outward and inward at the same time.

In Brussels, however, as the Six prepared to become the Ten following the decisive vote in the British House of Commons, and with Ireland, Norway, and Denmark also waiting to join, there were growing visions of a vast community far less concerned about the outside world.

Economists in Brussels pointed out that, in the enlarged Common Market, every nation would do between two-thirds and three-fifths of its trade within Europe.

The Europeans insisted that Treasury Secretary Connally was vague about what he expected them to do about trade —and that there was no chance of their pulling apart the Common Agricultural Policy or abandoning preferential arrangements to please the Americans.

Viscount d'Avignon said, "We cannot take one slice of the salami at a time, as the Americans would like, but must discuss the whole salami"—that is, discuss as well exchange rates, trade barriers, agriculture, aid to the underdeveloped countries, and military expenditures and American troop commitments.

He asked what sense it would make for Europe to go to great lengths to oblige the United States if American troops were pulled out of Europe in any case. But he conceded that an effort to deal with the "whole salami" might be a formula for failure. In the monetary area, he said, there are two possible routes ahead for Europe. One is to achieve an over-all settlement with the United States. The other is for a European solution alone, with a global reordering and fixing of exchange rates among the European currencies.

Echoing the warning of Chairman Arthur S. Burns of the Federal Reserve Board that "time is on nobody's side," de Strijcker said, "The longer the hesitation, the more likelihood that in one country after another people will demand actions to protect their economies." He added: "I see no cooperation on the United States side. Mr. Connally has taken drastic measures but he does not seem to realize that to succeed it is necessary to be open and frank."

There were also increased worries in Brussels about the future of American-European security arrangements. While asserting that the Nixon-Connally August 15 shocks would force them to come together economically, the European countries were lacking in confidence that they could unite to build an adequate conventional military force—and they saw no hope at all of achieving their own nuclear force.

Worried about their deteriorating relations with the United States, the Europeans have been looking with increasing eagerness toward closer economic and political relations with the Soviet Union as a means of affirming and safeguarding their existence.

A high French official tells the story of an American who ordered an apple pie in a restaurant but, when the waitress brought it, changed his mind. "I want a peach pie instead," he said. The American ate the peach pie and started to leave. The waitress stopped him. "You forgot to pay for the peach pie," she said. "Why should I?" asked the American. "I gave you an apple pie for it." "But you didn't pay for the apple pie," said the waitress. "Well, I didn't eat it, either," said the American.

To the French, the apple pie was the U.S. 10 per cent surcharge that the Americans wanted to use as bargaining material in exchange for currency upvaluations, trade concessions, and more military burden-sharing by the Europeans.

"There is no question of bargaining about the surtax," said Jacques Edin of France's Ministry of Finance. "There is no question of offering concessions for its removal. The surtax was taken by the United States in violation of GATT rules. It is not to be justified by the United States balance-of-payments deficits."

The French were being very hard-nosed. They said that the first thing to deal with was the monetary problem, and that this could be done only if the United States promptly removed the surtax. Then—at a later date—they would be willing to discuss trade matters on a bilateral or multilateral basis.

"But," said M. Edin, "this could occur only when the enlargement of the economic community has been completed." At the earliest, this would mean some time after January 1, 1973, when Britain and the three smaller candidates for Common Market membership—Ireland, Norway, and Denmark would be admitted.

As for military burden-sharing, French spokesmen said that since they were not military members of the North Atlantic Treaty Organization, this had nothing to do with them. They suggested the United States should take the question up in NATO.

Yet French spokesmen suggested that the United States might be able to make a deal on exchange rates that would not be too far off from what it sought—provided that President Nixon would be willing to devalue the dollar.

The French Government had taken the position that the value of the franc should not be altered—or, more precisely, as one official emphasized, "in no case should the franc be revalued vis-à-vis gold." This principle, he added, would still hold if the United States devalued in terms of gold. In other words, France would accept a U.S. devaluation without following the dollar down.

The United States believed that the key relations among the major currencies were as follows: The Germans would insist on having the mark 5 per cent to 6 per cent below the Japanese yen. The Germans would be willing to let the French franc and the British pound and Italian lira be about 5 per cent below the mark. The French, the British, and the Italians would be happier with at least a 7 per cent spread below the mark. But the wild card in the deck was the U.S. dollar.

If the dollar were not devalued, the French would almost certainly not upvalue—that was the whole point of their loudly proclaimed principle, "No change in the value of the franc vis-à-vis gold." And this would mean that the realignments the United States sought in the yen and the mark would not take place.

But if the United States were to devalue by 5 per cent in terms of gold, or in terms of Special Drawing Rights, which comes to the same thing, the major relationships could form something like the desired ladder. The yen could go up 10 per cent and be 15 per cent above the devalued dollar. The mark could go up about 5 per cent and be 10 per cent higher than the dollar. The franc, pound sterling, and lira would stay where they were and be 5 per cent above the dollar.

That was the deal France was modestly pushing, while insisting that her present situation was "not too bad," since, with the mark floating above 9 per cent, the franc had an even bigger advantage over her major Common Market rival, while France maintained a very tough system of exchange controls that protected her against speculative raids against the franc. Only 4 per cent of French exports go to the United States, so the surtax hurt them little, and they could afford to be patient.

French officials insisted that a U.S. devaluation was politically essential to resolving the crisis, though they conceded it has little economic significance whether the Americans devalued or they upvalued.

The United States was hoping to gain some leverage on the French through the Germans and had been hoping for much from the coming meeting between Chancellor Willy Brandt and Premier Georges Pompidou.

But a high French source said that Brandt and Pompidou had been "making progress," and added casually that he did not know whether the Brandt-Pompidou meeting would take place before the Group of Ten meeting in Rome in November or after it. He added that both Germany and France deplored Secretary of the Treasury Connally's postponement of the Rome meeting. But this might have been a smoke screen designed to conceal sharp conflict between the French and Germans over how far to go in meeting America's demands.

The Germans were more wary than the French about driving the United States out of Europe. They were afraid that, if the Europeans kept the dollar overvalued, they would compel the United States to take protectionist measures. A

U.S. retreat to isolationism and protectionism would undoubtedly damage all of Europe, including France through
the impact on her partners.

Nevertheless, a sharply critical attitude toward the United
States had become widespread in Europe. With recession
brewing and unemployment rising, there was less disposition
to yield to the Americans on the concessions originally
sought by Mr. Connally on exchange rates, trade, and defense.

Common Market officials and ambassadors of member
governments were talking more and more about making the
European Economic Community into a genuine political
entity with all the accoutrements of a state, including a defense force of its own. But, realizing that the Soviet Union
would never permit a West Germany rearmed with nuclear
weapons, the Europeans were seeking to build closer political
and economic relations with the Soviets.

American government officials were exasperated by the
stubbornness of the Europeans on the critical economic issues
and by their apparent inability to speak in one voice. Yet,
the message was getting through to the U.S. Government
that, like it or not, time was running out for a solution that
would avoid further deterioration in American relations with
Europe and Japan.

Every great political and economic event can be regarded
in two ways—as a unique turning point or as the repetition
of a historical pattern. In England, strewn with the monu-
ments of the past, people tend to see Great Britain's approaching entry into the European Common Market as a
re-enactment of history. *The New Statesman* saw Prime
Minister Edward Heath as Henry V about to launch his
forces against Agincourt, saying: "I see them stand like grey-

hounds in the slips, straining upon the start. The game's afoot: Follow your spirit, and upon this charge cry, 'God for Teddy, England, and the Common Market.' " And, as in Shakespeare's play, a love affair had developed between France and England in the chill autumn of 1971.

Queen Elizabeth said she would visit Paris in the spring. French Foreign Minister Maurice Schumann rushed to London to work out mutual plans for teaching French to the English and English to the French. It was all reminiscent of the charming scene in Act III, in which the French Princess Catherine, anticipating the arrival of Henry, asks her lady-in-waiting Alice for an English lesson, which winds up in blushing confusion. She doesn't know her foot from her elbow.

A few centuries later, the French have still not learned English, nor the English French, but the governments of both countries are ready to have another go at it. The French Government, having twice rudely vetoed Britain's application for membership in the Common Market, now wants the British in to help make weight against the Germans, who are increasingly the dominant economic power in Europe. The British Government, having seen all alternatives fade —the Empire, the Commonwealth, the special relationship with the United States—now sees Britain's future as inevitably moving forward into Europe.

Said a Whitehall figure, "Our retreat is ended. The colonies are gone. We have still five million people in the old colonial territories, but we cannot get rid of them. No one will have them. We are back where we started." And he added, in a line that could have been pure T. S. Eliot: "We are a medium power with medium ambitions."

Whitehall was already tooling up to send a strong force of British civil servants to the Berlaymont headquarters of the Common Market in Brussels. As a medium power, Britain was entitled to provide 20 per cent of the staff, having negotiated for parity with West Germany and France.

"We shall have two commissioners, one director general, and four or five directors," said a Whitehall official.

The question of reforming the Common Market bureaucracy is by no means a trivial one. *The Economist* has observed that the civil servants of Brussels were once the guardians of the "purest spirit of Europeanism" but are now

> declining into the status of a bureaucracy at bay; and one which feels that it can best recover its old power by creating and policing a series of restrictive agreements that may please lobbies of special interests—the common agricultural policy, a rigid system of unified exchange rates under a so-called European monetary union, rules against "unfair competition" and the like.

While *The Economist* bravely called upon the British Government to send men to Brussels who are entrepreneurial and innovatory in spirit—"and should on no account be ex-civil servants from Whitehall"—this seemed unlikely to happen.

Indeed, Whitehall already had a strong outpost in Brussels. One British officer posted there said, "In the colonial service our motto was, 'Wag the flag and flog the wog.' But now in the foreign service we say, 'Praise God, respect the Queen, and keep your martinis dry.'"

At worst, however, the British civil servants promise to add a cool sophistication and competence to the windy and pompous continental bureaucracy in Brussels.

While the British Government had its sails set for Brussels, the British people were still restless and unhappy over the crossing. Government officials did not dispute the results of a poll showing that more than 80 per cent of the public thought that Britain would enter the Market and that it would be good for the nation, yet almost 60 per cent remained opposed to British entry.

There appeared to be two basic reasons for the British public's continued sulking about the move into Europe. One was simply the expected rise in food prices. The British watch their pennies carefully and talk endlessly about what things cost. The government told them that, under the terms it had negotiated, food prices would go up only 2½ per cent per year, or 15 per cent in five years. But the people were skeptical; rising food prices have been the focus of people's annoyance over inflation. In 1971, unemployment was also rising. British economists expected the jobless rolls to pass the million mark, the highest level since World War II began.

The second reason for persistent popular opposition to the Common Market was political—a deep feeling that British sovereignty must not be infringed. One high government official scoffed, "The public didn't even know they had such a thing as sovereignty until this debate over the Market." But he conceded that vast sections of the public made their opposition to sacrifice of British sovereignty so loud and clear that the politicians—including Prime Minister Heath —had come to see the Common Market in much more restrictive economic terms than some of the earlier Tory rhetoric implied.

"At one time," said a government member, "it was thought that economic cooperation would lead to political union. But I do not expect to see this in my lifetime. It is at least several decades away."

"Whenever money is involved, *Gemütlichkeit* disappears," said Walter Scheel, the West German Foreign Minister, who had been seeking to rebuild a spirit of cooperation among the Common Market nations—toward each other and toward the United States. The Europeans were prepared to move a considerable distance to meet Secretary of the Treasury John B. Connally's terms—provided that the United States was prepared to make its own contribution to a monetary settlement. To the Europeans, the American contribution had to involve two elements: a devaluation of the dollar in terms of gold by 5 to 7 per cent, and an American agreement to drop the 10 per cent surcharge as soon as currencies were realigned.

The Europeans insisted that they were really not asking too much. They needed the dollar devaluation, they said, to quiet public opinion at home. But the real reason they needed it was to satisfy the French Government, which had planted its feet in concrete against changing the value of the franc in terms of gold. The French had said, however, that they would hold still for a moderate American devaluation.

The Europeans thought it only fair that the United States remove its import surcharge, since it had been adopted unilaterally in violation of American commitments to the General Agreements on Tariffs and Trade (GATT)—and described by President Nixon as a temporary measure.

Of all the European governments, the West German Government was ready to move fastest and farthest to end the threat of a monetary and trade war with the United States. The Germans regarded the economic issue as too important to be left to their economic and finance ministers —especially since Karl Schiller and Valery Giscard d'Estaing were involved in a bitter dispute that had become personal.

Chancellor Willy Brandt's meeting with President Georges Pompidou immediately after the Rome conference of the Group of Ten dramatized the importance West Germany attached to solving the monetary dispute promptly. "We cannot continue our detente with Eastern Europe," said Foreign Minister Scheel, "unless Europe's ties with the United States are strengthened."

The Brandt government's foreign policy has three interlocking elements: its *Ostpolitik,* which is aimed at normalizing relations with the Soviet bloc; its effort to build a closer political and economic union with the other Western European nations; and its determination to reforge the European-American alliance.

The Germans feared that any significant lessening of the American commitment to protect Europe would encourage the Soviet Union to step up its pressure on them. Indeed, the Germans were not alone in their fears that a withdrawal of American forces from Europe would be the prelude to a "Finlandization" of Europe.

Mr. Brandt was determined to do all he could to prevent a trade war from breaking out between Europe and the United States. In this he had the support of German industry. Aides to Mr. Brandt said that the German Government had felt no pressure from industry for retaliation against the United States. The Germans were willing to go far to oblige the Americans on the monetary, trade, and burden-sharing fronts to avoid serious damage to their foreign policy.

The French Government, however, was still dominated by Gaullist thinking. It was willing to risk a longer confrontation with the Americans. The Germans were seeking to avoid an open quarrel with the French. Mr. Scheel said, "France's first aim is to expand industrial production. Here in Germany, our main aim is economic stabilization—the checking of inflation. This yields differences in monetary policy. But we shall try to come to a common position."

There were deeper issues between France and Germany on economic policy. The Germans favored liberal international trade and a free-market economy. The French were more protectionist and more eager to use capital controls to maintain the stability of their currency. The French had become increasingly worried about the growing strength of the German economy. France's willingness to welcome Britain into the Common Market, after twice vetoing the British application, was widely regarded as evidence that France means to use Britain to help curb potential German dominance of the European Economic Community.

However, the Germans insisted that the *entente cordiale* between France and Britain "is not directed against us." The Germans were determined to keep their economy the strongest in Europe by halting their inflation—which had been running at about a 6 per cent annual rate, very high for West Germany.

The willingness of the West German Government to upvalue the mark was a key element in its strategy for blocking inflation. The upward valuation of the mark reduced the cost of imported goods and made more resources available for use within the German economy—both by encouraging imports and by discouraging exports.

Recession and rising unemployment in Europe as 1971 drew to a close were building pressures on all governments to move more quickly to resolve the monetary and trade confrontation with the United States. Likewise, on the American side, business uncertainties over the dangerous international monetary situation were increasing pressures on the Nixon Administration to work out an early settlement.

The international monetary game of "chicken" was growing too risky on all sides.

12. Alice's Dollar

The dollar was starting to shrink. At the Rome meeting of the Group of Ten major financial nations, in early December, 1971, Secretary of the Treasury Connally said the United States was willing to consider a formal devaluation of the dollar in terms of gold, that is, making it worth less in relation to gold and hence worth less in relation to the currencies of other nations. The once almighty dollar plunged to new lows on world currency markets.

Reacting to news of the sinking dollar—Connally asked the foreign finance ministers and central bankers how they would like a 10 per cent dollar devaluation—private businessmen and investors began selling dollars furiously. Foreign central banks, which earlier had insisted that they were already holding too many dollars, were forced to buy up hundreds of millions of additional dollars—more than they had accumulated in any week since President Nixon slammed the gold window shut on August 15, 1971.

But the New York stock market rallied strongly on the news, and American businessmen and investors said a dollar devaluation would greatly improve their hopes. And foreign securities markets rallied, too.

Secretary Connally, arriving back at Andrews Air Force Base outside Washington, declared that the Rome meetings had been marked by "warm and good feelings."

Essentially, what all this demonstrated was that fixed exchange rates among the world's currencies have lost their sanctity. The financial world had come to see it as folly for a nation to hold to a rate that forces it to run huge and chronic deficits in its balance of payments, as the United States had done for two decades.

The main aim of Mr. Nixon's monetary policy had been to force a realignment of the world's currencies with the dollar that would put the U.S. balance of payments into surplus. An overvalued dollar, the Administration, and a large majority of economists of all political colors agreed, had put too heavy a burden on American producers in international competition—including the competition for the huge U.S. market—because it made American goods expensive in comparison to foreign products.

Mr. Nixon's economists calculated that other nations would have to upvalue their currencies so as to produce, in effect, an average devaluation of the dollar by 15 to 16 per cent. This would swing the current American balance of payments by $13 billion (for example, from a $4 billion deficit to a $9 billion surplus)—the amount they figured essential to restore American strength. Every point in a devaluation, according to their estimates, would be worth $800 million to the United States.

But Washington still did not want to do the devaluing itself; it wanted other nations to upvalue against the dollar. Mr. Nixon and his aides contended that the dollar was the sun of the international monetary system, and the other nations were the moons, whose orbits could be changed.

But the other nations were no longer willing to accept this American concept of the system, which they regarded as archaic. With France leading the charge, they insisted on a direct dollar devaluation by Washington to prove that the dollar would be treated "like any other currency." France made clear that it would not upvalue the franc in terms of gold. In part, its stubborn refusal stemmed from an unwillingness to reduce the value of gold in terms of francs; the French bourgeoisie and peasantry are great gold-hoarders. In part, the French simply wanted to prove that the United States could be forced to do what others—especially France—had done when it was deep in deficit.

But as long as France held out against upvaluation, the Germans could not accord as large an upvaluation of the mark to the United States as the Americans wanted without according an excessive advantage to France, West Germany's hot competitor in the European Common Market. An American devaluation was essential to break this deadlock between West Germany and France.

Not only France but the other European countries as well were unwilling to accord the United States so big a swing in its balance of payments as $13 billion. Secretary Connally said that the United States "retreated" at Rome by proposing an 11 per cent net devaluation of the dollar, which would yield this country only about a $9 billion swing. Mr. Connally said this American concession "was not matched by steps of similar size" by other countries.

However, Mr. Connally as chairman closed the Group of

Ten meeting down before hard bargaining could test whether the distance between the United States and others could be closed. Some participants at Rome thought they were close enough to a deal that an all-night session plus an extra day of negotiations could have produced a realignment of rates.

But Mr. Connally ended the meeting and scheduled another one for Washington two weeks later. This session could follow summit meetings between West German Chancellor Willy Brandt and French President Georges Pompidou, and meetings between President Nixon and Canadian Prime Minister Trudeau and President Pompidou.

All of this summitry was why Mr. Connally was not ready to button up in Rome what must be regarded as Phase One of the international monetary solution. The Administration was determined to get foreign concessions on trade and a bit more on the exchange-rate side as well.

But the international monetary confrontation would not disappear even if Phase One—basically exchange-rate realignment, accompanied by a dropping of the U.S. 10 per cent surcharge on foreign imports—were concluded by the end of 1971. Phase Two, international division, would still involve protracted bargaining over tariffs, quotas, trade preferences, agricultural subsidies, border taxes, and other barriers to trade—in which both the United States and the others regard each other as the worst sinners. Phase Two would also involve struggles over military burden-sharing and over the amounts of American dollars that foreign governments are holding.

The rebuilding of the world's monetary system has scarcely begun. What is at stake is not only world prosperity but the power relations among the major Western powers and Japan. Mr. Nixon's summitry would be about matters of the highest policy—but it would be about money, too, which is as important to nations as it is to thee and me.

World attention had been so heavily focused on the struggle over the devaluation of the dollar and the revaluation of other currencies that some crucial economic issues involved in the confrontation between the United States and its trading partners and allies had been relatively submerged. The two most important of the submerged issues were: U.S. Government insistence that foreign governments start dismantling trade barriers to American exports; foreign concerns about the inconvertibility of the dollar into gold or other assets. Foreign central banks were already holding over $40 billion worth of inconvertible dollars and might have to acquire more.

On the first of these issues—lowering trade barriers against American goods—the United States wanted immediate satisfaction on some items plus a promise that foreign governments would commit themselves to a negotiation likely to result in a sizable improvement in the U.S. trade surplus.

First of all, the United States wanted some immediate "face-saving" concessions. One such concession would be over citrus fruits. In July, 1971, the Common Market, in a "unilateral gesture" to the United States, lowered its tariffs on citrus fruits from 15 per cent to 8 per cent during the four months of June through September—the months during which the United States, according to the Common Market, exports 85 per cent of its citrus crop. This reduced the preferential advantage which the European Economic Community had accorded to Spain and Israel. The United States wanted this citrus concession expanded and made permanent. It also wanted concessions on wheat; it charged that the Common Market, by its subsidy practices and failure to stockpile surplus wheat at times of temporary glut and distressed prices, was "dumping" and damaging U.S. wheat exports.

But citrus fruits and wheat were only the beginning. The Nixon Administration was preparing a new bombshell to shake the Europeans on the trade issue, and a hint of this had already been revealed in Geneva. It intended to submit a formal complaint to the General Agreement on Tariffs and Trade and might demand compensation for the damages to U.S. exports that had been done ever since the Common Market was formed in 1958. The bill of damages, insiders said, could amount to "several billion dollars." At the time the Common Market was established, the United States reserved the right to submit a claim for compensation on any damages caused by E.E.C. discrimination against American goods. It had finally begun to add up the bill. Some observers thought this was a bluff.

The United States particularly protested against the Common Market's preferential arrangements with third countries. When the E.E.C. was set up in 1958, it immediately negotiated preferential agreements with eighteen African countries and Madagascar. It later set up preferential deals with a group of Mediterranean countries—Greece, Turkey, Tunisia, Morocco, Spain, Israel, and Malta—and with three East African countries—Kenya, Uganda, and Tanzania.

Now, with the impending enlargement of the Common Market to include Great Britain, Ireland, Norway, and Denmark, the Europeans were planning to extend trade preferences to Switzerland, Sweden, Finland, Iceland, Portugal, and Austria, who seek only associate membership.

The Europeans asserted that the United States was being grossly unfair on the trade issue. They pointed out that the United States was still running a big surplus in its balance

of trade with Europe; the American trade surplus with the
Common Market was $2.4 billion in 1970. The Europeans
also offered data to show that U.S. trade with third countries receiving trade preferences had continued to expand.
But the Nixon Administration rejected these arguments,
contending that a bilateral trade surplus in no way justified
discrimination against U.S. goods.

Secretary of the Treasury Connally raised these issues in
Rome and reportedly felt that he was getting a runaround
from the ministers of finance who said that he should talk
to the Commission of the Common Market, and from a
representative of the Commission who said he should talk
to the ministers of governments. "If this goes on, gentlemen,"
Connally reportedly said, "you can choose your weapons."

The Europeans felt that the United States is at least as
guilty as they are of trade discrimination and protectionism,
and they said they would be willing to negotiate on a multilateral basis, if that were what the United States wanted.
But the United States wanted more than a vague promise. It
felt at a serious voting disadvantage in GATT, and it
wanted a commitment from the Europeans to accord what it
regarded as fair treatment. But skeptics regarded "fair treatment" as a euphemism for unilateral concessions.

The United States was not wholly without support for its
position on European preferences. West German Economics
Minister Karl Schiller, according to a high German source,
"is convinced that the preferences the Commission of the
Common Market has made on trade proposals are not in con-
formity with GATT." Dr. Schiller was described as having
the "American view."

But other Europeans have begun to fear that the Nixon
Administration no longer regards American interests as in
accord with further development of the Common Market.

West German Foreign Minister Walter Scheel said in Bonn, "By its decisions on trade policy, the United States may bring about the disintegration in the Western world." But the U.S. Government was unwilling to be deterred by such warnings from its determination to gain trade concessions. It concluded that the United States had been too soft too long.

President Nixon's announcement in the Azores that the United States had agreed to devalue the dollar strengthened hopes that the international monetary and trade confrontation would soon be over. President Pompidou was pleased.

France had been in no hurry for a realignment and was ready to hold out longer. The French had gained a great advantage from the currency realignments that had already occurred during the preceding two years—especially from the upvaluations of West Germany, France's most important competitor and customer.

In those two years, the French franc had been devalued by 30 per cent relative to the West German mark. This enabled the French economy to advance well on the basis of a strong export performance, while West Germany and other European economies had been slowing down and suffering from rising unemployment.

With West Germany and France at odds not only on the values of their currency but also on the European common agricultural policy, plans for a European monetary union, and other issues, a Common Market crisis had been superimposed on the international monetary crisis. In these circumstances, the United States had been unable to overcome French resistance or extract significant immediate trade concessions from the Common Market.

France was in the driver's seat in the Common Market.

Less concerned about the American market than West Germany and other European countries and less concerned about the U.S. military role in Europe, France had been relatively immune to American pressure.

The President's decision to devalue came right on the heels of Secretary of the Treasury Connally's statement that "there has been no commitment on our part to make such a decision."

But there remained many other outstanding issues facing the United States and its trading partners that would continue to bedevil the international scene.

The trade issue was at the top of the list. Said a leading businessman, Frazer B. Wilde,

> We are going to have a continuing problem on the trade balance, as I see it. Some of our major specialties, such as airplanes and electronics, will be a reduced factor in the future in producing exports. The agricultural situation is outrageous. Politically we can do little about it. We have exported enough technology, machinery, and mass production know-how to seriously affect shipments from our country. Whether the dividend return through foreign earnings will grow enough and fast enough to balance it, is difficult to determine.

At least as important as the trade issue was the future convertibility of the dollar. This was at the heart of the issue of how to construct a new world monetary system to replace the Bretton Woods system that President Nixon abandoned when he slammed the gold window shut on August 15, 1971.

In a sense, Bretton Woods had been abandoned years earlier. Most countries knew perfectly well that they could not freely cash their surplus dollars in for gold or other reserve assets in the United States. But they could maintain that fiction for home consumption until August 15.

In actuality, other countries knew they were on a dollar standard—and they did not like it but feared to do anything about it.

Now foreign countries wanted to end the dollar standard; it gave the United States a privilege that they were no longer willing to accord it—the privilege of running whatever debts the United States wanted abroad and covering them with paper dollars, without negotiating with anyone and without accepting discipline on its balance of payments. Not only did this give the United States a free hand in foreign policy and in capital investment abroad, but it made the growth of world reserves subject to the policies and economic developments within one dominant currency country.

This meant that if the United States ran big payments deficits, either because of low interest rates or inflation or foreign military activities or any other reason, world currency reserves would grow too fast and inflation result. But if the United States swung too suddenly from deficit into surplus, world monetary reserves would cease to grow or even shrink, forcing deflation and unemployment upon other countries.

The Nixon Administration had every intention of keeping the dollar inconvertible in terms of gold or other assets for the foreseeable future. The great majority of American economists thought this was a wise and necessary policy; they said it would only throw the world back into monetary turmoil for the dollar to go convertible prematurely, while the United States had inadequate gold reserves to meet outstanding claims and had no assurance that its balance-of-payments deficit would promptly disappear.

However, it would be dangerous to keep the dollar inconvertible and still try to maintain a world dollar standard, if most other currencies were fixed and most countries wished to return to a fixed-exchange rate system. This could inflict serious damage on economies abroad and trigger foreign reactions that would seriously hurt wide segments of the American economy as well.

Aware of such dangers, well-informed businessmen and economists warned against premature euphoria on the solution of the international monetary and trade confrontation.

13. "I Have No Enemies"

Only a few weeks before the Washington monetary agreement, when the economic crisis was at its grimmest, a European statesman compared the United States to the Florentine prince who, as he lay dying, was asked whether he did not wish to confess his sins. "I have nothing to confess," he replied. Then did he wish to forgive his enemies? "I have no enemies," he said. "I killed them all."

Many European leaders were alarmed at the ruthlessness of the American economic offensive. The Italian finance minister, Mario Ferrari Aggradi, said he had been warning his counterparts in other countries all along that it was a stupid mistake for the Europeans to put the United States in a corner over its payments deficits—because there would be a "terrible reaction" from the Americans. "And without the United States," he said, "Europe is over."

But the French Government, dominated by Gaullist think-ing, less concerned about keeping its share of the American market or keeping American troops in Europe, was deter-mined not to yield to Secretary of the Treasury John B. Connally's demands that Europeans upvalue their currencies and grant the United States major trade concessions. The French insisted that there could be no settlement without United States "participation" through a dollar devaluation and trade concessions of its own. President Pompidou prides himself on what he has called his "obstinacy."

It looked as though the immovable Frenchman had met the irresistible American. Yet, at the Azores summit meeting between President Pompidou and President Nixon, a deal was made according to which the United States agreed to de-value the dollar by 8 per cent and remove the import sur-charge, in exchange for what Mr. Pompidou regarded as minor trade concessions and a nebulous agreement to discuss but not necessarily do anything about major long-term issues, such as Europe's common agricultural policy.

What caused Mr. Nixon to yield? Basically two forces— the first most prominently represented by Arthur F. Burns, Chairman of the Federal Reserve Board, and the second by Henry A. Kissinger, Mr. Nixon's chief foreign policy ad-viser.

Dr. Burns, who had already demonstrated that he could stand his ground and win against massed White House op-position in the area of wage-price policy, warned the Presi-dent that a protracted international monetary crisis could have a devastating effect on the U.S. money and security markets—and on the American economy generally. A num-ber of prominent businessmen and bankers concurred. The President, whose re-election doubtless depends on a healthy economic recovery, was shaken.

Dr. Kissinger's concern was that Secretary Connally's aggressive policies, if pressed too far, would finally force Europe and Japan to counterattack, jeopardize U.S. relations with its principal allies, and weaken national security. Mr. Nixon's scheduled summit meetings with Prime Minister Trudeau, President Pompidou, Prime Minister Heath, Chancellor Brandt, and Premier Sato gave Dr. Kissinger the handle he needed to take hold of the monetary and trade confrontation.

Mr. Trudeau went back to Ottawa almost ecstatic: He had been subjected to domestic political criticism for not shielding Canada from the American economic offensive. Mr. Pompidou gained a victory about which he could crow modestly. And Mr. Heath, without acrimony, was able to let Mr. Nixon—and Mr. Pompidou—know that Britain's old "special relationship" with the United States had been transmogrified into a "normal relationship."

Considering the heavy constraints under which he was operating once the President began to listen to Dr. Burns and Dr. Kissinger, Secretary Connally still played his cards boldly and came off with a bigger currency realignment than had been expected. But whether he made significant progress on the trade issue is doubtful. He tried to hang on to as much leverage as possible by inserting into the Washington accord a provision that the President would not ask Congress to devalue the dollar in terms of gold until he had a package of trade concessions that would withstand congressional scrutiny. Although he received the plaudits of the crowd, Secretary Connally had taken a hard blow from the President during the Azores summit meeting. Some observers thought he had had his bargaining position spoiled by the President —and that he himself had been harpooned. Only a few weeks later, Mr. Nixon indicated that Spiro Agnew would be his running mate in 1972; Mr. Nixon didn't want to break up a "winning team."

Mr. Nixon billed the Washington accord as the "most

significant monetary agreement in the history of the world," and indicated that the United States would cooperate in building a more open and competitive world trading system.

However, it was too early to conclude that Mr. Nixon had now switched decisively to a more liberal foreign economic policy. There were still powerful political forces in Congress and in the nation's industries and labor unions for protectionism. There was strong suspicion within the Administration about the European Common Market—a belief that it is increasingly becoming a threat rather than a boon to American economic interests. President Pompidou publicly attacked what he regarded as an American effort to eliminate the common agricultural policy—and, implicitly, the European Economic Community itself.

Mr. Nixon's self-labeled Nixon Doctrine was based on the recognition that the United States no longer held so predominant a political and military role as it did during the first two decades after World War II. This doctrine had its economic corollaries, but the question was whether the loss of American predominance implied a foreign economic policy more aggressively self-interested ("Like any other nation's," said an Administration official) or a policy that recognized the need for greater equality or partnership and cooperation with other major economic powers. In this area, as in many others, Mr. Nixon appears to like ambiguity.

William L. Safire, special assistant to President Nixon, told a *New York Law Journal* forum that the first of the great changes he foresaw for 1972 would be a "growing awareness of the economic root of international power. Our eyes will become accustomed to the new Big Five in world affairs—the United States, the Soviet Union, the Common Market, mainland China and Japan." What do these portentous words mean? Are they simply inflated rhetoric or do they signify a coming development in U.S. foreign economic policy whose importance has not yet been appreciated?

The Safire statement repeated a theme that the President himself voiced in Kansas City, Missouri, July 6, 1971. Mr. Nixon then declared that there were "five great economic superpowers"—the same named by Mr. Safire—that would "determine the economic future and, because economic power will be the key to other kinds of power, the future of the world in other ways in the last third of this century."

"We now face a situation," said Mr. Nixon, "where the four other powers have the ability to challenge us on every front, and this brings us back home for a hard look at what we have to do."

Domestic and foreign policies were so intertwined, he said, that they could not be separated. Mr. Nixon warned that the United States was reaching the period of "decadence" that had brought down Greece and Rome. In the past, he said, decadence had resulted from growing national wealth. This had caused earlier great civilizations to lose "their will to live, to improve." But he thought the United States had the strength and courage to meet all challenges.

In that Kansas City speech, delivered only five weeks before the President launched his New Economic Policy, he linked national health and strength to the free-enterprise system. He delivered a strong indictment of wage-and-price controls, declaring that such steps were alien to the American system of free enterprise. Mr. Nixon then froze wages and prices and subsequently adopted Phase Two controls.

But, at the December, 1971, American Economic Association convention in New Orleans, Professor Paul Samuelson predicted that the Administration would end wage-and-price controls before the November, 1972, election. And Assistant

Secretary of the Treasury Edgar R. Fiedler said that the best time to get rid of wage-price controls would be before the economy gets back to full employment.

Since Administration economists apparently regard a rate of unemployment of 5 per cent as tantamount to full employment, rather than 4 per cent as was customary in the past, this could mean suspending controls almost any time in the coming year, assuming even a modest decline in unemployment from the recent 6 per cent rate.

President Nixon himself, in a television interview, said that the Johnson Administration's low unemployment rate had been achieved "at a cost of 300 casualties a week" in Vietnam; but he would continue to wind the war down.

Declaring that his system of wage-price controls was intended "to break the inflationary psychology," Mr. Nixon also took issue with a statement of Paul W. McCracken, former chairman of his Council of Economic Advisers, that wage-price controls might be needed for years to come.

The restatement of the "five great powers" theme might foreshadow a return by the President to the true free-enterprise creed in 1972. But this need not mean a diminution in White House support for aids to business, especially in the international arena. Peter G. Peterson, assistant to the President for International Economic Affairs, who succeeded Maurice H. Stans as Secretary of Commerce, suggested a number of additional government aids to business, including help on research and development outlays, exemption from the antitrust laws if needed to spur exports, and a value-added tax, with rebates for exporters.

The foreign economic policy implications of the "five great powers" concept do not all go in the same direction. Toward the Common Market and Japan, the concept appears to mean the sort of tough and highly competitive attitude expressed frequently by John B. Connally and by Mr. Peterson. But toward the Soviet Union and mainland China —foes though these countries may be in the Communist world—Mr. Nixon has adopted a friendly view and has stressed his hopes for growing trade. United States–Soviet relations, he said in his Kansas City speech, have moved from confrontation to negotiation. And he added that he had moved to end the isolation of Communist China, because that country had become "creative and productive."

In straight economic terms, it is difficult to see United States trade with Communist China amounting to a great deal for years to come. Despite its enormous population of between 750 million and 850 million, China's gross national product is estimated by Western experts at only about $80 billion—about 7 per cent of this country's. China's exports are chiefly textiles, agricultural materials, and foodstuffs.

Peking has signaled its interest in trading with the United States, although it can get most of what the United States could offer elsewhere—for instance, in Japan or Western Europe. Nevertheless, China would doubtless like to get certain American products because of their superior quality. The significance of Mr. Nixon's interest in developing trade with China was certainly more political than economic. The same holds for his plans to increase U.S. economic relations with the Soviet Union.

Thus, the "five great powers" concept implied that Mr. Nixon was heading into a year of important economic maneuvering among the other four great powers. The curious thing was that this champion of the free-enterprise creed appeared to be working for closer economic relations with Communist China and the Soviet Union as he toughened his response toward the growth of economic power in Western Europe and Japan.

14. After the War Is Over

In May, 1970, when the stock market came close to a full collapse—not on the news that the war might end but on the threat that the Cambodian invasion might lead to a major escalation—the ambassadors from Wall Street to the White House effectively conveyed to President Nixon the warning that fear of a widening war was threatening to produce a financial panic. This was an important factor in his reiterated pledge to get U.S. troops out of Cambodia by the end of June.

Beyond the financial community, broad segments of the society were calling for a shift of national priorities. There has, in fact, been strong competition between Mr. Nixon and the Democrats over who will get the credit for shifting the balance of the federal budget from military to social expenditures.

Many people are skeptical or even cynical about this belated desire to liquidate a dirty, unprofitable, and unwin-
nable war. Even some defense contractors would now like to
see the war in Vietnam ended, because it wastes billions on
troop pay, transportation, and combat operations, starving
the federal budget for funds to pay for major weapons programs.

There is no reason to suppose that most nondefense industries link their economic interests with those of defense
producers. Since businesses with little or no stake in the
defense budget see that they must transfer resources to
defense industries via taxation and suffer from cost inflation
and damaged markets that cut into their profits, they have
come increasingly to identify their own best interests with
peace rather than war.

Yet it is all too obvious that particular centers of defense
production—such as Seattle or Southern California—can be
hard hit by defense cuts. Local dependence on military production needs to be made obsolete by government willingness to plan substitute kinds of expenditure or to make
other provisions for readjustment of the industrial mix. This
may not be easy to do, but it can be done. Fiscal policy, in-
volving expenditure hikes or tax cuts, and monetary growth
can keep total national demand for goods and services high
enough to avoid unemployment and economic stagnation,
in the judgment of the great majority of economists, conservatives and liberals alike.

The long postwar record of economic growth and full (or
overfull) employment of Western European countries and
Japan, whose military budgets are a minor fraction of that
of the United States in relation to national income, shows
that peace and prosperity in capitalist societies are by no
means impossible to attain.

But there is inertia against changing the existing industrial mix of the American economy; it is the task of political leadership to overcome that inertia.

The Soaring Sixties came to an end with the bear market of 1969–70, the failing stockbrokers, the shakeout of the conglomerates, the Penn Central fiasco, the empty feeling of the airlines, the sinking spell of aerospace and electronics, the climb in unemployment, and the emergence of the up-tight consumer and businessman.

Was this the end of a war boom—and the end of an era? Hyman P. Minsky of Washington University thinks it was —and that the Soaring Sixties have given way to the Sluggish Seventies. His thesis is that the longest economic expansion in U.S. history, stretching from early 1961 until late 1969, has altered the structure of the financial system, decreasing its stability and dampening its vibrancy.

Professor Minsky contends that the liquidity crisis of 1970, like earlier financial crises, has put a mark on the economy that will last through much of the decade. He holds that all deeply depressed business cycles of the past were associated with a financial crisis, and all mildly depressed cycles were not, and he regards the misery of 1970 as a financial crisis.

In their monetary history of the United States, Milton Friedman and Anna Schwartz note that four of the six most severe cyclical contractions—1873–79, 1893–97, 1907–8, and 1929–33—were marked by banking crises and financial panics, which resulted in a deep drop in the money supply. In the two other severe contractions—1920–21 and 1937–38—they attribute the drop in the money supply to deliberately foolish actions by the Federal Reserve System.

But private bankers can behave as foolishly as central bankers. The Friedman-Schwartz history reveals that the collapse of the Bank of United States, which triggered the most catastrophic banking crisis of 1930–31 and did much to intensify and prolong the Depression, could have been prevented but was not—because of social prejudice.

New York's State Superintendent of Banks, Joseph A. Broderick, and Lieutenant Governor Herbert Lehman had desperately appealed to the establishmentarian members of the Clearing House Association to save the Bank of United States, which was known as a "Jewish bank."

Superintendent Broderick later recalled:

> I said it had thousands of borrowers, that it financed small merchants, especially Jewish merchants, and that its closing might and probably would result in widespread bankruptcy among those it served. I warned that its closing would result in the closing of at least ten other banks in the city and that it might even affect the savings banks. The influence of the closing might even extend outside the city, I told them.
>
> I reminded them that only two or three weeks before they had rescued two of the largest private bankers of the city and had willingly put up the money needed. . . . I warned them that they were making the most colossal mistake in the banking history of New York.

Mr. Broderick's warning did not impress Jackson Reynolds, president of the First National Bank and of the Clearing House Association, who told Broderick that the effect of the closing would be only "local."

The reform of the banking system, especially through the creation of the Federal Deposit Insurance Corporation, removed such decision-making from the members of a private club.

Since the crash, we have built a floor under monetary contractions, not just by insuring bank deposits but also by a willingness on the part of the federal government to incur huge budget deficits and on the part of the Federal Reserve to pour massive monetary reserves into the banking system in periods of acute financial stress.

But, according to Professor Minsky, although we have raised the floor under the money supply, our economy is still subject to the downward pressures that follow a great boom. The euphoria of the boom, he says, increases the willingness of businessmen to invest and "emit liabilities" independently of the rate of growth of the money supply. But the rapid growth in demand leads to tight money markets and to escalating interest rates—and inflation. The effort to stop inflation by checking the growth of the money supply finally breeds a liquidity crisis.

The Federal Reserve System has the means of shifting direction to head off a full-scale financial crisis. This is precisely what Chairman Arthur F. Burns and the Federal Reserve Board did during the spring and summer of 1970. But, although the central bank may rescue the economy from deep crisis, it cannot prevent tensions and tremors from passing through the business world and from changing the spending, investing, and saving propensities of individuals.

Will the end of the Vietnam war lift the spirits of the American people and dispel anxieties about the Sluggish Seventies? Or will it aggravate anxieties and cause a postwar slump?

President Nixon has blamed much of the rise of unemployment in the United States in 1970 and 1971 on the "winding down" of the Vietnam war. And Secretary of the Treasury Connally has described as a "myth" the 4 per cent unemployment rate used by economists, Republican and Democratic, as equivalent to full employment. "It has never happened," said Mr. Connally, "save in wartime, not in the last quarter of a century."

Similar worries troubled the nation when World War II was ending. In 1945, the United States had 11.4 million men under arms. By 1946, the armed forces had been reduced to 3.4 million, in 1947, to 1.6 million, and in 1948, to 1.46 million—a postwar slash of ten million men who had to be absorbed into the private economy.

What happened to unemployment in the first full year of peace a quarter of a century ago? In 1946, there was a brief readjustment, but unemployment during the first postwar year still averaged only 3.9 per cent. In 1947, the unemployment rate held at 3.9 per cent, and in 1948, the rate went down to 3.8 per cent. The great postwar depression, so widely feared by Keynesian economists, never materialized.

On the contrary, the coming of peace in 1945 and the huge drop in military spending ushered in a boom. While military spending was dropping from 42 per cent of gross national product in 1944 to 4 per cent of GNP in 1948, after-tax profits of American business more than doubled, rising from $11.2 billion to $22.7 billion. It helped to launch a great wave of business expansion.

What had happened was that the American public, in the bliss of peace, cashed in its wartime savings, borrowed heavily, married, had babies, bought homes and cars and other goods at a great clip, and drove business to invest and invest in new plant and equipment.

To be sure, World War II was an all-out affair and may have scant relationship to the economic impact of more limited wars, such as Korea and Vietnam. In 1950, the year the Korean war broke out, corporate profits after taxes totaled $24.9 billion. By 1952, profits were down to $19.6 billion. Then, in 1953 and 1954, years affected by a recession owing in part to cutbacks in post-Korean defense spending, after-tax profits averaged $20.5 billion annually. And in

1955, profits after taxes climbed to $27 billion. In 1954, the first full year after the Korean war, unemployment averaged 5.5 per cent, but in the three peacetime years that followed, the unemployment rate was 4.4 per cent in 1955, 4.1 per cent in 1956, and 4.3 per cent in 1957. This period of solid prosperity ended with the sharp 1957–58 recession, which was unrelated to war or postwar factors.

The late Wesley C. Mitchell, founder of the National Bureau of Economic Research, used to say that every business cycle was unique. He might have added that every war is unique as an economic phenomenon.

Vietnam has certainly been unusual in one unquantifiable way—its impact on the emotions of the American people. Probably no war has had so depressing an effect on public morale. The way the war came and was waged created a mood of public distrust, most marked among the young but eventually shared by a large part of the population of all ages.

The war has been a drain on the economy in every sense— unlike World War II, which lifted a depression-ridden economy up to full employment. By contrast, in 1965, when President Johnson began his major escalation of the war, the economy was already close to full employment. This meant that resources for waging the war could come not from idle capacity and manpower but at the expense of civilian production.

The direct costs of the war in Indochina have exceeded $100 billion. But the total costs—without even trying to put a dollar figure on the loss of life and casualties resulting from the war—have been much greater. As Robert Eisner of Northwestern University has put it, "The list of war costs reads like a catalog of evils and suffering in the American economy." The war has caused inflation; it has caused high taxes; it has contributed to housing shortages; it has drained resources from education, transportation, housing and all the services of government, from police protection to postal delivery. Probably the greatest indirect cost of the war is that, in producing inflation, it has brought on government monetary and fiscal policies to check the inflation that have resulted in a serious loss of output and real income for the entire society.

Robert J. Gordon of the University of Chicago has estimated that, even if the American economy were to climb rapidly from now on and regain full employment by the end of 1972 (defining full employment as 3.8 per cent unemployment, the standard earlier set by President Nixon's Council of Economic Advisers), the recent economic slump would have caused a loss of $100 billion in output. This heavy loss would have been incurred to achieve an inflation rate that, at best, in 1971–72 would be only 1 percentage point less than the rate would have been if unemployment had been held at 3.8 per cent from the fourth quarter of 1969 onward, according to Professor Gordon's estimates.

He calculated that a policy to hold the unemployment rate at its early 1971 level of about 5 per cent for another two years to "beat the inflation out of the system" would cost an additional $171 billion in real output, with only a bit more short-run effect on prices but no long-run effect on inflation.

Professor Gordon concluded that, whatever rate of unemployment the Administration sought, the best strategy was to promote as rapid a recovery as possible to that target, because any delay would not alter the eventual rate of inflation associated with a given unemployment target. Since the price slowdown associated with a more sluggish recovery is only temporary, he contended, it would not be worth prolonging the agony in higher unemployment and lost output.

But will the end of Vietnam really mean the transition from a wartime to a peacetime economy? The Joint Economic Committee of Congress was highly dubious that there would be any such transition—at least measured in terms of total military expenditures.

Noting that President Nixon had asked for $80.2 billion in budget authority for national defense in fiscal 1972, a $6 billion increase over 1971, both Democratic and Republican members of the Joint Economic Committee stated: "This indicates that the Administration plans to resume the upward trend in defense spending in the near future." The Committee insisted that "it is difficult to see anything peacetime about an $80 billion defense budget."

The Committee strongly suspected that the Administration was using its military budget to prop up the domestic economy. "If it is the policy of the Administration to relieve the unemployment problem by increasing defense spending," the Committee declared that it would be "in strong disagreement with that policy."

Instead, it called for reductions in defense spending—"in the interests of national security"—through reform of weapons procurement to eliminate cost overruns, the "gold-plating" of weapons, and other wasteful defense practices. The committee wanted an economic conversion program, focused on social objectives rather than a policy of converting outlays on manpower and shooting-war needs into garrison-state expenditures, especially military hardware, as a means of achieving full employment.

The Joint Economic Committee contended that the war and a high level of defense spending had contributed to an inflationary psychology. Although the expectation of inflation, in traditional economic theory, is supposed to lead to an immediate rush of buying, this need not be so; such a buying rush did occur during the first weeks of the outbreak of the Korean War, but the sluggish behavior of consumers during the last years of the Vietnam war, as inflationary expectations continued to strengthen, demonstrated that consumers do not automatically rush to buy ahead of price increases. Indeed, consumers could be acting quite rationally when they cut their buying because of inflationary expectations. They might decide that price increases of goods they need would outrun their ability to raise their incomes, and hence that they must cut back on their discretionary purchases of such things as automobiles and television sets.

Further, as inflation pushes up interest rates, it increases the rewards for saving. Fear of unemployment—a potential result of government and Federal Reserve efforts to check the inflation—can also impair consumer confidence and spending. The Joint Economic Committee went so far as to assert that "the consumer's confidence will not fully return so long as the debilitating and demoralizing effects of the war in Southeast Asia persist."

Investors react to war-generated inflationary threats in much the same way as consumers. The sickening plunge of the stock market in the spring of 1970 was a direct reaction to the Cambodian invasion and to fears of a wider war, bigger government spending, bigger deficits, more inflation, escalating interest rates. The President's campaign to steady the stock market involved efforts to convince the business community and the public that Cambodia was a limited maneuver to shorten rather than widen the war.

But will an end to American involvement in the war in Vietnam necessarily produce a great wave of national confidence and euphoria? President Nixon himself has suggested that, depending on how the war ends, it might instead give rise to bitter national recrimination and dissension. Such a national mood would not only aggravate social and economic tensions at home but could hurt U.S. relations with other countries. It would very likely intensify already evident signs of neo-isolationism.

After World War I, the late John Maurice Clark of Columbia University wrote:

> In international affairs, the sequel of the War in this country seems to have been an increasingly stubborn insularity, resisting an inescapable trend toward sharing in world affairs. The fact that this resistance is less strong on the eastern seaboard may be a mitigating factor, or it may only be a cause for the development of an ill-omened sectionalism between the eastern seaboard and the interior.

Evidence of conflict between the so-called Eastern Establishment and Middle America has been all too apparent for some time. It was a major theme in the Presidential candidacy of Senator Barry Goldwater, and it has been a strong element in the politics of President Nixon and Vice President Agnew. On the economic side, it found its echoes in the "get tough" policy toward other nations of Secretary of the Treasury Connally.

A generation ago, J. M. Clark found that America's postwar insularity included "a thoroughly thick-skinned attitude as to what other peoples think of us." He saw this attitude as a kind of defense mechanism; America felt that it had lost something of its reputation and sensed this in foreign reactions to America's determination to collect the war debts, in foreign aversion to what came to be regarded as excessive investment of American capital in their countries, and to retaliation against intensified American protectionism in trade. "We have not been very actively loved in the past, perhaps," Professor Clark wrote, "but now we seem to be actively resented, for reasons not difficult to understand."

The United States, he said, had not felt enough of the misery of World War I to make us appreciate what others had borne and suffered; even our economic and material burdens were light relative to our strength. He implied that the nation was suffering from feelings of guilt.

The most important things about the war for America, said Professor Clark, were "the imponderables," the way it affected the national psyche. Basically, the war had been a calamity, though with some compensations:

> we have learned things, as men must from any great experience; but too often we seem to have learned the wrong things. And we might have had better experiences to learn from. Perhaps all we can be sure of is that nothing has remained untouched by the War. Everything that has happened has happened differently because of it.

J. M. Clark was writing from the perspective of 1931. How will we see the Vietnam war and its impact on the course of American history from the perspective of 1984? Obviously, much depends on how we use our economic knowledge—such as it is.

15. The Black Art
of Economics

Many people apparently believe that economics would not be such an awful subject if economists would just stop being so obscure, pedantic, and boring. Laymen who would like to see an increase in economic literacy, including their own, often ask economists to state some simple, basic economic truths that everyone should be taught. This is not as easy as it sounds, but it is worth trying:

• There is no such thing as a free lunch.
• The price system allocates resources, determines what is to be produced and for whom with marvelous efficiency and fairness, if you assume perfect competition and perfect mobility of all resources, and if you possess a social philosophy like that of Herbert Spencer or Commodore Vanderbilt.

• When the investments that businessmen intend to make exceed the public's intended saving, economic activity will increase; and when the saving that the public intends to do exceeds the investments that businessmen intend to make, economic activity will decline—provided that all terms are defined in a way that will support these conclusions.

• An increase in the money supply will cause an increase in prices and/or business activity, especially if you go to the University of Chicago.

• Real income will grow if productivity increases, provided that the real income referred to is that of the society as a whole and provided that productivity increases under circumstances in which the real income of the society as a whole is increasing.

• Happy is the land that knows balance-of-payments equilibrium, reasonably stable but flexible prices, reasonably full employment, economic efficiency, a good income-distribution in some sense, and a growth rate that is probably greater than zero but not so rapid as to deplete resources and pollute the environment, provided that this is the will of the people and that the will of the people is assumed to be the appropriate mechanism for determining the society's welfare.

• Government should do for the people only what the people cannot do or cannot do so well for themselves—all the words in this proposition being defined in any way anybody likes.

• Competition is invariably better than oligopoly or monopoly, if the world is static, if existing technology is appropriate, if there are no industries with increasing returns to scale, and if you dislike all forms of socialism or realism.

• To solve a general and nonstructural unemployment problem, either increase demand or get new unemployment statistics or redefine unemployment; to cure a noncost-push inflation, either reduce demand or get new price statistics or redefine inflation.

• Finally, lest you think this is cheating, let us consider the basic economic truth that value in exchange is a differential function of value in use, which simply means, as the distinguished economist P. H. Wicksteed carefully explained, that:

> what a man will give for anything sooner than go without it is determined by a comparison with the *difference* which he conceives its possession will make to him, compared with the difference that anything he gives for it or could have had instead of it will or would make; and, further, that we are generally considering in our private budgets, and almost always in our general speculation, not the significance of a total supply of any commodity—coals, bread, or clothes, for instance—but the significance of the difference between, say, a good and a bad wheat harvest to the public, or the difference between ten and eleven loaves of bread per week to our own family, or perhaps between ten days and a fortnight spent at the seaside. In short, when we are considering whether we will contract or enlarge our expenditure upon this or that object, we are normally engaged in considering the difference to our satisfaction which differences in our several supplies will make.

In other words, we consumers substitute a bit more of certain goods that now cost less than they did for certain other goods that now cost relatively more than they did, provided that our incomes are constant, that we read *Consumer Reports,* that we are not too lazy or stubborn or habit-prone or happy, that we are mercenary and do not know the people with whom we do business and have no interest in trading our high-priced dogs for their high-priced cats, that we have time and wit to make all the relevant calculations, and so on. Brushing aside all such complexities, however, we may safely assert, as Wicksteed puts it, "that the differential theory of value in exchange asserts that value in exchange is value in exchange," while "all other theories assert that it is not."

To summarize: In the great cafeteria of economic understanding—or understandings, as the professional educators say—there is no such thing as a free lunch.

Honest economists, including both those who have and who have not committed themselves to teaching economics to children and the general public, know that economics is an unusually tricky subject; so do unusually intelligent noneconomists. As Keynes recalled:

> Professor Planck, of Berlin, the famous originator of the Quantum Theory, once remarked to me that in early life he had thought of studying economics, but had found it too difficult! Professor Planck could easily master the whole corpus of mathematical economics in a few days. He did not mean that! But the amalgam of logic and intuition and the wide knowledge of facts, most of which are not precise, which is required for economic interpretation in its highest form is, quite truly, overwhelmingly difficult for those whose gift mainly consists in the power to imagine and pursue to their furthest points the implications and prior conditions of comparatively simple facts which are known with a high degree of precision.

The economist, on the contrary, is used to dealing with a great deal of information that comes to him in imprecise form. Even if he gets numbers that look clean, he knows that they are only shadows of a world that is anything but neat, precise, orderly, systematic. He knows that he must try to impose order on a disorderly mass of information as his normal job. Other scientists may have to do this in the beginning of their science or may have to do it at crucial turning points in its development, but thereafter they are filling in parts of an empirically solid structure or, in the case of mathematics, of a logically consistent structure. The economist must do essentially what an artist or writer does (although he is not so impressionistic or subjective as these): He must apprehend reality freshly every time he confronts it; he is constantly working from life, unless he has gone utterly stale.

To be sure, the economist has a secret weapon that other people do not have: economic theory. This gives him certain habits of thought that enable him to conceptualize problems that he has not seen before or problems that seem always to confront him in a new way. This is what keeps economics exciting for those who like it and what makes the economist —when he is good—such a handyman. He is able to apply his concepts to problems that, to the noneconomist, may seem totally unrelated to one another—the strategy of conflict, the farm problem, the growth of an industry, the decay of a region, the improvement of public health. All such problems are challenges to the economist's ability to cope with interdependence—and poor data.

The basic bits of economic theory seem simple, obvious, even trivial. Every child realizes without being taught that if a good is cheaper, he is likely to buy more of it. But what is missing for the child is the over-all system, the mode of analysis, the analogies among all types of economic activities and problems; this is what makes it so hard to teach economics to others. One gets it by doing, not by listening.

The economist develops through a kind of quasi-Talmudic training: long on discussion and debate, with continuous passage from the specific to the general and back again; savagely close in its textual criticism; skeptical about its own or anyone else's results; complicated and wide-ranging in its style of inquiry. Calvin Bryce Hoover and Joseph J. Spengler, as teachers, always stressed that economics could never be a monologue art, that the economist always needed to try his reasoning on some other economist. This is probably generally true. It also probably explains why the economics profession is so strong and close a fraternity. The economic monologue artist is not only out of touch but in danger of becoming a crackpot or, less seriously, a layman.

Yet economists as a class often seem crackpot to laymen. Between Christmas and New Year's, when most rational human beings huddle within the bosom of their families or fly off to a Caribbean island or a Vermont ski lodge, thousands of American economists assemble in stuffy halls and listen to one another read papers that are every bit as fresh and several times more comprehensible when they are published five months later. At the end of 1970, for instance, the economists spent Christmas vacation reading their papers to each other in Cobo Hall, even better known as the home court of the Detroit Pistons.

What basketball players and economists have in common is that they are in it for the money, the prestige, the fame, and the thirst for victory over the competition. Among both of them there are doubtless some pure artists, who simply love the games—the city game and the academic game. But economics is a miserable spectator sport, poorly understood by most nonplayers. As Walter Salant has noted, most laymen think that what economists do is to forecast the stock market and the business trend. Actually, the majority of economists are involved in studying a much wider range of matters, such as the structure of the labor market (including the hard-hit academic job market), television, the rising cost of health care, urban growth and congestion, the economic barriers to blacks and other minority groups, the political economy of environmental quality—all of the above being a small sample from the Detroit program of the economists.

Other sessions dealt with foreign trade and the less developed countries, political decentralization, graduated work incentives, education and worker productivity, Soviet planning, intergeneration transfers of wealth in this country, male-female wage differentials, pollution, population growth, inflation and the distribution of income, demobilization after Vietnam, and teaching economics to black students. If anybody thinks economics is not "relevant"—the great educational cliché of our time—it is certainly not because economists aren't trying.

The retiring president of the American Economic Association, Professor Wassily W. Leontief of Harvard, said that the real problem is not that the economists are not shooting at relevant targets (he agreed that the fire should shift as the targets move), but that they are just not hitting anything. The reason they are missing, he said, is the "palpable inadequacy of the scientific means" with which economists try to solve problems. They do too little work developing data; they underrate the importance of observation in science. He blamed the economics profession for bestowing its honors, in vastly disproportionate degree, on abstract theorists and model-builders, rather than upon empiricists. Professor Leontief, whose own fame derives from his invention of the input-output system of analyzing national economies, is singularly unimpressed with the contribution of beautiful mathematical models to the solution of dirty, complicated problems.

As it happens, though, Professor Leontief's successor as

president of the American Economic Association, Professor James Tobin of Yale, once described himself to President Kennedy, who wanted him for his Council of Economic Advisers, as an "ivory-tower economist." J.F.K. said that was fine, because he was "an ivory-tower President." The remark, though ironic, said much about the intellectual tone of the Kennedy Administration.

At Cobo Hall, the third top member of the hierarchy was Professor John Kenneth Galbraith, who became president-elect and program chairman for the 1971 Christmas paper-reading.

Professor Galbraith had to forego the skiing at his beloved Gstaad in Switzerland to get to Cobo Hall, where he might have been mistaken for an aging Piston center. Where Professor Leontief has criticized the economists for a lack of empiricism, Professor Galbraith blasts them for a kind of mental retardation—that is, for compulsively working on what he regards as stale and outmoded problems, such as economic growth. The real problem today, says Professor Galbraith, is not how fast we can increase production and consumption, but how well—how happily—we are to live.

"Even you tend to associate happiness with expenditure," Professor Galbraith recently scolded a young English reporter, Frances Cairncross, daughter of an eminent British economist, Sir Alec Cairncross, "it's a habit—something you picked up from the economic textbooks."

"In a rational life-style, some people could find contentment working moderately and then sitting by the street—and talking, thinking, drawing, painting, scribbling, or making love in a suitably discreet way," Professor Galbraith told the young lady. "None of these requires an expanding economy."

Dispatched to India as ambassador while the New Economists were in the saddle in Washington, Professor Galbraith is happily having his innings in the new age of pollution. And the economists, excoriated by Professor Galbraith for years, hailed him as their 1972 president. It is difficult to say whether this is a sign of total security or insecurity on their part. It is more likely an expression of approval of Galbraith's effort to restore richer social, moral, and aesthetic qualities to a profession that has been showing signs of becoming desiccated by technical scholasticism.

The fear of rigor mortis is, in fact, a worry that economists today have in many countries. A recent review, in the *Economic Journal* of Britain's Royal Economic Society, says of Lionel Robbins: "He is one of a very small number of contemporary economists who still maintain the tradition of economics as a humane discipline." "Growth and stability" is the old battlecry of the economics profession. But the motto for the economists' convention at Cobo Hall was: "There is nothing stable in the world; uproar's your only music."

Nowadays, it is not just Professor Galbraith who has deserted raw growthmanship; more and more economists are coming to feel that the most important, unsolved problem facing their profession is how to reduce or prevent the undesirable consequences of growth—such as choked highways, overcrowded airports, noise, foul air, polluted water, despoiled nature, urban sprawl, decaying central cities, and the damaged central nervous system of human beings.

Radicals contend that such effects are endemic in the capitalist system. However, Charles L. Schultze, who was Director of the Budget in the Johnson Administration and is now a Senior Fellow of the Brookings Institution, points out that the ugly by-products of growth are present in Communist as well as capitalist systems.

Industrial societies often push economic growth at the expense of the environment not because of some "giant conspiracy of capitalist moguls"—or of Communist bureaucrats—but because the signals and incentives built into either system ignore the costs of pollution.

In this country, for instance, a chemical plant may save money by dumping effluents into the river but add to the costs of those downstream that need clean water. Plants and factories that befoul the air pass part of their production costs on to society in the form of higher health bills and lower property values.

The economist's jargon for such cost transfers is "negative externalities."

But there are also favorable externalities. Businesses that design and build well help to restore a community. Companies that train and employ disadvantaged workers relieve the financial burdens of taxpayers generally.

Society may hurt itself by not taking account of externalities. That was the theme of the movie *Quackser Fortune Has a Cousin in the Bronx*. Quackser, a poor Irishman, followed milk-wagons around Dublin, sweeping up the horse manure and selling it to housewives for their gardens. Motorized milk trucks drove out the horses and put Quackser out of business.

But a correct calculation of the externalities—the favorable ones like lovely gardens and happy housewives, versus the negative ones like air pollution and a grimmer city—might have kept Quackser Fortune and the horses in business and the motorized trucks out, provided that there had been an appropriate system of rewards and penalties, forcing polluters to "internalize the externalities."

To be sure, the calculation of who is a polluter and who

is a social benefactor is far from simple; some people don't like horse manure.

Despite such complexities, however, the search is on among economists for new and workable systems of social rewards and penalties to augment or correct the private marketplace's calculation of costs and profits.

Here are some of the proposed "analogs of the market," as Mr. Schultze calls the new social signals and incentives, that would guide the actions of both private and public decision-makers:

• Effluent charges for pollution control.

• Incentive contracts in manpower-training programs.

• Efficiency-oriented reimbursement schemes in medical insurance programs.

• Experimental voucher schemes, individual student aid, and performance-oriented pay scales for teachers, as a means of stimulating educational bureaucracies.

• Mandatory flood insurance, with premiums adjusted to flood risk as a method of inducing rational flood-plan development.

• Charging the military budget for the current cost of atomic weapons and the present value of currently accruing veterans' benefits, as a means of inducing more rational resource allocation.

• Providing military decision-makers with incentives to avoid "gold plating" of weapons—that is, choice of the most expensive kind of military hardware where the extra power is not worth the cost.

• Designing grant-in-aid programs with more flexibility and with incentives for mayors and governors to bargain with the federal government about the best mix of local grants.

• Adopting a system of congestion charges for airports to spread traffic, reduce delays, and provide investment signals.

The attempt to solve such social problems will require a tremendous effort on the part of economists to make their arid science more humane. How radical a transformation will this involve?

16. Is Economics Out of Date?

Two centuries ago, Edmund Burke proclaimed, "The age of chivalry is gone. That of sophisters, economists, and calculators has succeeded; and the glory of Europe is extinguished forever." But is the age of the economists already coming to an end? In highly industrialized societies, concepts of human well-being are changing; will the science of economics therefore also undergo profound change?

At the height of the Victorian era, the great systematizer of economic thought, Alfred Marshall, said it was the business of economics to examine "that part of the individual and social action which is most closely connected with the attainment and with the use of the material requisites of well-being." Marshall contended that man's character has been molded by his everyday work and the material resources that he earned "more than by any other influence unless it be that of his religious ideals; and the two great forming agencies of the world's history have been the religious and the economic."

Here and there, the ardor of the military or the artistic spirit has been for a while predominant; but religious and economic influences have nowhere been displaced from the front rank even for a time; and they have nearly always been more important than all others put together. Religious motives are more intense than economic, but their direct action seldom extends over so large a part of life. For the business by which a person earns his livelihood generally fills his thoughts during by far the greater part of those hours in which his mind is at its best; then, his character is being formed by the way in which he uses his faculties in his work, by the thoughts and feelings that it suggests, and by his relations to his associates in work, his employers or his employees.

Marshall's thought was not narrow, cramped, or materialistic. Yet he shared the faith of the nineteenth century that an increase in the production of material goods would mean an increase in the well-being of society as a whole.

That faith is fading fast in the second half of the twentieth century. Louise Curley has noted that American economists were close to the mark in forecasting the rate of growth in the 1950's and again in the 1960's, but that what their data measured had little relationship to the most significant changes in the well-being of the American society. The economists had generally failed to anticipate the deterioration of the environment stemming from rising production, population growth, and technological advance. They had not foreseen the impact of rapid economic change on America's cities—how fast the rot would spread at the center; how much crime and drug addiction would grow;

how fast the middle class would flee to the suburbs; what violence, riots, and burnings would come.

Neither the economists nor the generals nor anyone else could have imagined at the start of the 1960's that the United States, with its enormous economic strength and military power, could have failed to prevail in the longest war in its history over what seemed to be a tenth-rate Asian power. The cost in lives and broken bodies has been terrible, but in that respect, Vietnam is not different from other wars. What is new for the United States is the blow to national self-regard—and the blow to the national image of what constitutes greatness.

We may indeed be on the brink of Mr. Nixon's "new prosperity—without war or inflation." Yet the feeling will not die that, with the disappearance of inflation and unemployment, the nation's deeper problems will not be solved.

The worrisome lesson of the past decade is that economic growth and full employment do not go to the heart of what ails the United States. The welfare problem, racial polarization and conflict, drug addiction, crime and violence, the decay of cities, and the decline of civility all worsened in the midst of full employment. Nor did these ills disappear with the increase of unemployment at the start of the 1970's.

Where is the economics that can address itself to the deeper needs of the American society or of other highly industrialized nations and begin to cope with the wastage of human resources that only begins with unemployment?

Economics needs a more realistic conception of human well-being than one so closely tied to data on output and income that it leads society toward self-destructive goals.

Statistics on earnings tell us little about the condition of man; Thomas Carlyle argued in 1839:

> The condition of the working-man in this country, what it is and has been, whether it is improving or retrograding,—is a

question to which from statistics hitherto no solution can be got. . . . one is still left mainly to do what he can ascertain by his own eyes, looking at the concrete phenomenon for himself.

He admitted this was a most imperfect method but felt that it was the only sound method and that each man must take what he has seen with his own eyes as a sample of all that is seeable and ascertainable.

"What constitutes the well-being of a man?" Carlyle asked. He was willing to include as elements the wages a man gets, the bread his wages buy, and the steadiness of his work. But these, said Carlyle, were only the preliminaries:

Can the labourer, by thrift and industry, hope to rise to mastership; or is such hope cut off from him? How is he related to his employer; by bonds of friendliness and mutual help; or by hostility, opposition, and chains of mutual necessity alone? In a word, what degree of contentment can a human creature be supposed to enjoy in that position? With hunger preying on him, his contentment is likely to be small! But even with abundance, his discontent, his real misery may be great. The labourer's feelings, his notion of being justly dealt with or unjustly; his wholesome composure, frugality, prosperity in the one case, his acrid unrest, recklessness, gin-drinking, and gradual ruin in the other,—how shall figures of arithmetic represent all this?

In our time, the problems of using economic arithmetic to measure the condition of "labourers" are probably even more difficult than in Carlyle's. Our "labourers" include not only the active labor force—employed or unemployed—but millions on welfare, prisoners, criminals, and quasicriminals who get their living "on the street."

Our "acrid unrest" derives from barriers of race as well as social class. Our social conflicts, air, water, and noise pollution, and traffic congestion afflict not just the bottom but the whole of society.

Nowadays, "gin-drinking" must stand as metonym for many forms of drug abuse. "Recklessness" causes tens of thousands of deaths every year—with the automobile an even worse instrument of death than the hand-gun.

But it is true that we are richer, live longer, know more, or at least go to school longer, work fewer hours, play more or passively sit more, absorbing entertainment.

Some scholars are seeking to develop social indicators to set beside the economic indicators as measures of well-being and guides to social policy. The problem of quantification is incredibly difficult, because well-being is a complex cultural bundle, not a series of discrete phenomena. Is well-being necessarily increased if people have longer vacations but the highways are choked and the beaches overcrowded? More may not be better, but less is not better either—if it means less health, less freedom of movement in the city, less land, less friendship.

But individuals want very different things. Many really want big, fast cars, electric appliances and gadgets, the pleasures of Las Vegas or the numbers racket in Harlem, the hunting of animals. Is it possible to reconcile the existing range of subjective preferences with the well-being of all? What degree of freedom is optimal for mankind? Thomas Jefferson offers one view, Fyodor Dostoyevsky another, Jean Paul Sartre a third, Albert Camus a fourth, Milton Friedman a fifth, John Kenneth Galbraith a sixth, Leonid Brezhnev a seventh, Mao Tse-tung an eighth, and so on.

The radical economists of the New Left have leveled a heavy attack on the welfare concepts of neoclassical economics. Herbert Gintis, a member of the Union for Radical Political Economics, writes: [1]

[1] Herbert Gintis, "Neo-Classical Welfare Economics and Individual Development," *Occasional Papers of the Union for Radical Political Economics*, 3 (July, 1970), 16–17.

But neo-classical welfare economics
Does not claim
To be a general theory.
Rather,
It claims to be correct
Within its own realm of application.
That is,
It does not claim to be able to handle
All aspects of individual welfare,
But limits itself
To those aspects which involve
Marshalling scarce resources toward the satisfaction
Of competing ends.
To deal with the problem of individual development,
According to this contention,
One must address a different theory—
such as some theory of psychology or philosophy or
religion or social relations.

But most economists today would maintain that neo-classical economics is simply a set of analytical techniques, applicable to certain aspects of production, distribution, exchange, consumption. They would assert that economics aims at increasing the efficient use of resources but cannot specify goals for society or prescribe ways in which individual preferences should be developed or controlled.

The radicals hold that this "separation scheme" of the economists is unjustifiable; they reject "efficiency economics," even within its own limited area of application. They contend that the professedly cool and neutral economists have indeed put their mark on capitalist society, which, in aiming at efficiency and the growth of production, builds institutions that shape individual preferences to further the attainment of those economic goals.

Professor Galbraith, a distant cousin of the radicals, particularly inveighs against advertising as the key institutional means for molding individual preferences to make possible achievement of the corporate goal of expanding production.

But both Professor Galbraith and the radicals would say that it is not only advertising that furthers the goal of maximizing the growth of the private sector of the economy including not only business managers or stockholders but workers as well. In the mixed economy, the story grows more complicated as politicians, government officials, and local and regional interests get into the act.

The so-called military-industrial complex is a case in point. As Adam Yarmolinsky says, the military-industrial complex is not a conspiracy but "there are coincidences of interest among the military project officer who is looking for a star, the civilian who sees an opening for a new branch chief, the defense contractor who is running out of work, the union business agents who can see layoffs coming, and the congressman who is concerned about campaign contributions from business and labor as well as about the prosperity of his district." Under Mr. Nixon we had a brilliant example of this process in the bail-out of the Lockheed Aircraft Corporation—and not on a military project but on the civilian airbus, the L-1011.

It is no longer only the radical economists or Professor Galbraith who are challenging the traditional blandness of economics on social goals or its mindlessness about the impact on society of profit-maximizing business activity.

More and more economists—including conservatives as well as liberals—are coming to feel that the most important unsolved problem facing their profession is how to reduce or prevent the undesirable consequences of economic growth.

Some nonradicals point out that the ugly by-products of industrial growth—pollution, despoiled nature, urban sprawl and decay—are present in Communist as in capitalist societies. One approach to reducing or eliminating those by-products is by imposing direct social controls, another is by developing new signals and incentives, such as tax breaks or penalties, subsidies or uses charges, to encourage private behavior that better conforms with social goals.

Many conservative economists feel that their most important job is to try to prevent the political process from acting perversely and reducing social welfare. They would rather let the private market operate in its unadulterated form than have government move in to subsidize private ventures, when there are what economists call "negative externalities"—damage to the rest of society.

That is why many economists joined in the battle this past year against the government subsidy to have a supersonic transport (SST) airplane produced. Almarin Phillips of the University of Pennsylvania, an economist who has long been a student of the aviation industry, found little merit in the argument that there would be a social loss if the United States were not the first nation to fly an SST commercially.

The United States, Professor Phillips said, had not been first with fabric and metal trimoters, nor with low-wing, all-metal monoplanes, nor with subsonic jet transports. The SST, he said, was almost certain to be unprofitable.

The balance-of-payments and employment arguments for the SST, said Professor Phillips and the large majority of economists outside government, were specious; there are better and less costly ways of achieving these goals.

Finally, said the economists, agreeing with the environmentalists, there were very grave possibilities of external costs from sonic boom and pollution of the upper atmosphere, endangering the health of people on earth.

There is no need for economics to cease to be economics in order to contribute to other social goals than increasing efficiency or maximizing output. Although it is obviously not their unique talent, economists have something to contribute in helping society to formulate goals more rationally. In the pursuit of more intelligent and humane goals, the economists' respect for data and analytical skills can often be extremely effective.

The growing concern among economists with "micro" problems, such as pollution, the use or misuse of public money to subsidize the maritime industry, the aircraft industry, the highway-building industry, agriculture, and many others, the uses or abuses of government regulation of transportation, communications, power, securities markets, and other fields will probably intensify the heat and fog of battle in which economists play their public role. In time, a deeper understanding by economists and the public of such microeconomic problems may do as much to serve society as has greater knowledge of macroeconomic ailments, such as depression and mass unemployment.

In addition to the effort to widen the social perspectives of economics, a quite different critique is coming from some social scientists who are concerned about the constricted and out-of-date methodology of what they call "conventional economics." Conventional economics is the science of choice; it is orderly, definite, and linear, like classical music. Here, says the professor of conventional economics, are the factors of production—land, labor, and capital. Each of these is not a lump but a homogeneous string of units. The job of the economic theorist is to tell the decision-maker how to combine these elements to maximize something—efficiency or production or short-term profits or long-term profits.

This minute shifting of interchangeable resources at the margin, say the critics, was all well and good in the old days, when it was possible for the economist to take technology as given and to regard his own task as juggling with existing resources. But what happens to economics when research, technological change, innovation, knowledge, and new ideas —as well as finite bits of land, labor, and capital—become the factors required to increase productivity? The focus then shifts from the neat strings of factors of production to the complex and unique human personalities involved and—in a corporate world where the creative process is institutionalized—to large-scale human organizations.

Hence, argue the critics of conventional economics, the walls of economic theory must be broken down to let in the other social sciences. Instead of the old simplifying psychological assumption that man is a pain-pleasure, profit-loss calculating machine, economists must look more profoundly at the question of what really makes man tick, alone and in groups. They must find better ways both of improving human beings ("investing in human capital" is the cliché for this) and of improving human performance. In a society where people increasingly are separated from the traditional land-labor-capital nexus and do intangible things—researching, conceptualizing, advising, writing, thinking, feeling, innovating, imagining—the distinction between productivity and creativity blurs.

The general attack on problems of human thought and action is breaking down the barriers not only between economics and the other social sciences but also between the social sciences and natural sciences. Herbert Simon of Carnegie-Mellon University regards the narrow specialization of disciplines over the past couple of centuries as a "regrettable consequence of the population explosion among words." So-called experts, he says, can scarcely talk seriously with anyone outside their own narrow fields, except about "personal" matters.

Perhaps the most exciting prospect of change resulting from the new theory and technology of information-processing, Professor Simon suggests, is that it will halt and reverse this progressive isolation of idea from idea and man from man. "Mankind, in its professional as well as its nonprofessional aspects, will again become the proper study of man," he said.

But it is not just the research revolution in general, nor the coming of the computers in particular, that explain the shaking up of conventional economics; rather, it is the coming together of the streams of rapid methodological advance in the social sciences and growing concern about problems that simply cannot be solved by conventional economic approaches—such as how to eradicate poverty and other social ills in underdeveloped or highly developed countries.

Economists once thought that, to bring a backward economy into the modern age, the essential job was to transfer gobs of capital to it. This has turned out to be a laughably inadequate answer. The range of social, psychological, educational, organizational, managerial, political, and even moral complexities involved in economic development has shattered the simplistic assumptions of conventional economists.

Similarly, the persistence of poverty and the worsening of many social and environmental problems in rich, populous, industrial societies have forced economists to question the adequacy of their tools for improving human welfare—the classic aim of economics.

Whether, because of these powerful forces coming to bear upon it, conventional economics will collapse and undergo radical change remains an open question. Professor Martin Bronfenbrenner of Duke University doubts that this will happen soon. He observes that moderately unconventional economists—especially when nobody is baiting them—regard their own work as a desirable supplement to conventional economics and express their hope that, in the future, economists will pay more attention to current work in psychology, sociology, and political science. But a few extremists, says Professor Bronfenbrenner, "including my colleagues when you or I are nasty to them, propose to displace conventional economics by 'economic sociology' or 'behavioral economics' the day after tomorrow." Bronfenbrenner himself is pragmatic about the issue. If the new behavioristic economics works better than the old stuff, he says, so much the better—and if the new computer-aided, man-is-the-proper-study-of-mankind approach is "not economics," as conventional economists maintain, then so much the worse for economics. It would certainly have been no devastating criticism of modern psychology for phrenologists to insist that it was not phrenology.

Thus, after a long spell of quiet and even smugness about the state of their science, economists are asking themselves tough questions about what they should be doing and how. This may turn out to be important for solving some of the perplexing and stubborn problems afflicting this nation and many others. It may ultimately have a great deal to do with how men and nations can be helped to behave more humanely and sensibly, with less harm to one another.

Perhaps some danger exists that economics—a limited field but one with some significant achievements behind it —will drown prematurely in a sea of related disciplines before it has adequately solved some of its own traditional problems, such as how to simultaneously achieve full employment and price stability and how to put together a stable, essentially free, and expanding world economy. But efforts to solve even those traditional economic problems can only be advanced by a deeper understanding of many matters that lie beyond the boundaries of conventional economics.

17. Serene Detachment

The philosopher Baruch Spinoza, referring to his work on politics and ethics, wrote: "I have sedulously tried to deal with the subject of this science with the same serene detachment to which we are accustomed in mathematics." In his masterpiece, *History of Economic Analysis*, Professor Joseph A. Schumpeter said that every economist ought to be able to repeat that sentence of Spinoza's on his deathbed. Achieving serene detachment is next to impossible for the economist in government, but the ideal is a worthy one.

The Nixon Administration's economists did not demonstrate much detachment from politics in interpreting the economic indicators as the economy slid into recession. In fact, they stubbornly refused to concede that a recession had occurred at all. On September 24, 1970, speaking at the fiftieth anniversary of the National Bureau of Economic Research—the independent center for economic analysis that has long been regarded as the authoritative score-keeper of cyclical expansions and contractions—Herbert Stein of the C.E.A. sharply criticized the contention of Professor Solomon Fabricant that the American economy might be in a "growth recession." Dr. Fabricant, a long-time member of the National Bureau and its former re-search director, had presented a long paper to show that, in a modern, growth-oriented economy, a drop in the rate of expansion could be just as traumatic as the sort of abso-lute economic contractions that in the past had been called "recessions."

Professor Fabricant subsequently decided that a recession had in fact begun in November, 1969. Indeed, he found that the economy had been in not just a "growth recession" but an absolute recession.

In 1971, the economy continued to advance, but unem-ployment persisted. Seasonally adjusted unemployment had been only 3.5 per cent of the civilian labor force in Novem-ber, 1969. Unemployment rose to 6.2 per cent by January, 1971, and continued to oscillate about 6 per cent through the remainder of the year.

The sluggish growth of the economy in 1971 was not what Mr. Nixon's economists had predicted. They had forecast a gross national product of $1,065 billion for 1971 —a figure that the large majority of private economists re-garded as incredibly high—and the private economists proved to be right. Before the year was half over, the Council of Economic Advisers had disowned the $1,065 billion fore-cast. This high forecast had been primarily the result of analysis conducted in the Office of Management and Budget, based on a monetarist model of the American economy, created by a young economist, Dr. Arthur Laffer, on leave from the University of Chicago. In the debate over the year's forecast among the O.M.B., the Council of Economic Advisers, the Treasury, and the influential Budget Director, George P. Shultz, had prevailed. Dr. Shultz made the O.M.B. model available to *The New York Times*. He explained that only so high a rate of growth as the $1,065 billion forecast implied would be consistent with acceptable progress in reducing unemployment.

Although the Council of Economic Advisers was later to insist that the $1,065 billion forecast was "its own," the annual economic report of the Council cautiously noted the "considerable body of opinion that expects the gross national product for 1971 to be in the range between $1,045 billion and $1,050 billion." This, said the C.E.A., "is a possible outcome. However, it seems more likely that with present policies the outcome would be higher than that and could be as high as $1,065 billion." Such a level, it added, "would be consistent with satisfactory progress towards the feasible targets of an unemployment rate in the 4½ per cent zone and an inflation rate approaching the 3 per cent range by mid-1972."

The American economy refused to follow that script. Inflation did not seem to be fading away—and the White House, still determined not to drop its floundering game plan, fiercely attacked its critics.

The White House was eager to stop Chairman Arthur Burns of the Federal Reserve Board from continuing to press for a stronger incomes policy—and it struck at him and the Board. Close observers in Washington suggested that the White House not only wanted to put pressure on Dr. Burns to stop saying that it was not doing enough to check inflationary wage-and-price increases, but also wanted to dissuade the Federal Reserve Board from arresting the very rapid growth of the money supply; the White House wanted to embarrass Dr. Burns, "either to diminish his impact on public opinion or to force him to resign and make room for a more docile central bank head." [1] A Presidential aide [2] called in a reporter from *The Wall Street Journal* to say that Mr. Nixon was seriously considering making legislative recommendations—in which many of his principal advisers concurred—to bring the Federal Reserve into the executive branch.

The White House aide said that the President was "furious" with Dr. Burns for continuing his public campaign for a wage-price review board. The "final straw," he said, was Dr. Burns's appearance before the Joint Economic Committee on July 23, 1971, when Dr. Burns said there hadn't been "any substantial progress" against inflation. The President was tired of hearing from bankers and businessmen that "the great Arthur" was contradicting Mr. Nixon's assertions that the economy was recovering satisfactorily with considerable progress against inflation, said the aide.

Then the really dirty smear was applied; the aide charged that the Chairman of the Federal Reserve Board was being "hypocritical" about inflation because he had been "trying to get his own salary raised from $42,500 to $62,500."

A Federal Reserve spokesman, when asked about this, said that Dr. Burns "hasn't requested any salary increase,"

[1] *The Wall Street Journal,* July 29, 1971, and October 15, 1971.

[2] The White House aide was DeVan L. Shumway, a member of the staff of Herbert G. Klein, Mr. Nixon's Director of Communications, who was doing the job on Burns under the direction of Charles Colson, the President's "hatchet man," defined by Presidential aide William L. Safire as "an insider who does the dirty work for a public figure." Mr. Colson also participated directly in leaking the story of the possible Administration assault on the independence of the Federal Reserve to the press.

but declined further comment. Presidential Press Secretary Ronald L. Ziegler passed up chances to disavow the personal assault on Burns. But by the end of the week, a White House official was saying that the earlier "leaks" about Burns were "not a legitimate expression of Presidential opinion." [3] And Mr. Nixon himself said that Dr. Burns had received an unfair "shot."

The assault on Chairman Burns and the independence of the Federal Reserve Board had provoked an extremely hostile reaction to the White House from the business and banking community—and apparently hurt the stock market, a mood indicator to which the White House is highly sensitive.

Businessmen, economists, and statisticians have reacted unfavorably—but timidly—to Administration moves to ensure that the Bureau of Labor Statistics presents a picture of the economy in harmony with the rose-colored views of the Nixon Administration's political leaders. President Nixon and Secretary of Labor James D. Hodgson were determined to curb or get rid of Harold Goldstein, the veteran Assistant Commissioner of the Bureau of Labor Statistics for employment and other manpower statistics, and some of his assistants—as well as others within the Bureau who supported them, such as Peter Henle, the chief economist, who was also reorganized out of a meaningful job—because these career economists would not make public statements interpreting the figures as their bosses wanted them to.[4] In addition, the Administration has eliminated some reports that give unwelcome facts, such as poverty-area and detailed unemployment data that show very high rates of joblessness among central-city blacks and teenagers.

[3] *The New York Times,* July 30, 1971.
[4] See particularly Eileen Shanahan's articles in *The New York Times,* October 9 and 10, 1971.

Heavy political pressures—and occasionally a muzzle—were also applied to economists at the Commerce Department and even at the Council of Economic Advisers, to bolster the Administration's claim that business was picking up and inflation subsiding, during the months prior to the big switch in Nixonian economic policy.

But the facts were stubborn, and it became increasingly clear that a switch in the game plan was coming.[5] Budget Director George P. Shultz staved off the change at the first Camp David summit conference during the last weekend of June, 1971. His victory—which Secretary of the Treasury Connally manfully proclaimed—proved extremely short-lived. After the President finally decided to throw in the sponge on the old game plan, some Administration officials were willing to say how inevitable the change had become. Deputy Director of the Office of Management and Budget Caspar W. Weinberger, who took part in Camp David II, said there were ample signs of the coming change—as when twelve Republican Senators on August 5 asked the President to consider wage-price controls.

Since World War II, the American political system has made room at the top for academics—economists and other scientists—who have achieved their positions of great influence not through the elective process but because their specialized knowledge is regarded as a valuable national resource, to be institutionalized in such bodies as the Council of Economic Advisers. However, if the knowledge of the academics is not exercised disinterestedly, professionally, and in the interests of the broad society rather than a particular party leader, they will finally lose both their influence

[5] "It May Be Time to Change the Game Plan Again," *The New York Times*, "The Week in Review," Sunday, June 27, 1971.

and their claim to public respect. By the same token, politicians who bring undue pressure upon their professional advisers or career economists and statisticians are guilty of desecrating a national resource.

18. The Economics of Richard Nixon

After the New Economic Policy was launched, an interviewer asked John Ehrlichman, the lawyer who serves as President Nixon's chief assistant for domestic affairs, how much of the Camp David economic program could be attributed to John Connally, the Democratic politician from Texas. "Oh, I think a substantial amount," said Mr. Ehrlichman. "Going back to the June weekend, there was pretty much unanimous consent at that time that nothing should be done. But the Secretary urged a readiness to activism then. I think that was very influential." [1]

By the time the President and his advisers were ready to go to Camp David for the second economic conference in mid-August, had George Shultz been persuaded that all of

[1] *National Journal,* October 2, 1971, p. 1994.

the program that eventually emerged was advisable? "Yes," said Mr. Ehrlichman. "The disengagement from gold was the one big open question—although not with George who favored it—and it remained an open question until Saturday or possibly early Sunday morning. The President had had George come and explain the program to me (excepting the gold question) the previous Tuesday, and he was very much in favor of it at that point."

John Connally led the discussions at Camp David II, was chairman of the working staff group, was at the head of the table in Laurel Lodge, and, said Mr. Ehrlichman, "pretty much chaired the meetings." In pushing for the New Economic Policy, had Mr. Connally stressed the political aspects? "It was certainly one of the things he stressed, but he wasn't the only one by any means," said Mr. Ehrlichman. "There were some old Nixon hands who also measured the political realities of the situation."

But it was the failure of the monetarist economists to deliver the promised results that finally caused the politicians to blow the whistle on the original game plan. When it was over, a few of the economists did some Monday-morning quarterbacking. Paul McCracken, the day before his departure from his office as chairman of the Council of Economic Advisers, said he was less "Friedmanesque" than he had been three years earlier. He now thought that expansion of the money supply was a necessary "accompaniment" of an expansion of production and jobs, but he was doubtful that money-supply growth, brought about by actions of the Federal Reserve System, would by itself produce expansion of the economy. Dr. McCracken "essentially" supported President Nixon's decision for "full-employment balance" in the fiscal 1973 budget, but he conceded that there might be a case for a full-employment *deficit* to stimulate the

economy in the coming year. Looking backward, Dr. Mc-
Cracken said he thought that there were areas where he now
thought action might have come earlier than it did. One was
the swing away from a restrictive, anti-inflation budget and
monetary policy, which he thought should have come sooner
than the spring of 1970, given the long lags. He would have
switched sooner, if he had it to do over again, to the move
to control wages and prices. But for such a wage-price control program to work, he said, "you need a broad base of
public support. . . . You have to wait until the people are
virtually demanding the program before it has a good
chance to succeed."

And, in the presence of his colleagues at the American
Economic Association, Professor Milton Friedman considered the question of whether monetary policy had failed.[2]
It depends on what you mean by failure, he said. During
the Great Depression of 1929–33, monetary policy had failed
in the sense that the economic physicians had prescribed
the *wrong* drugs—a reduction in the money supply—but the
drugs had "worked," and the economy collapsed.

During the first three years of the Nixon Administration,
said Professor Friedman, "I believe that the monetary policy
followed, while much closer to the correct policy than from
1929 to 1933, was deficient," because the monetary authorities had let monetary growth swing from one extreme to the
other. In the two years before January, 1969, he said, the
money supply defined as M_1 (demand deposits and currency
in circulation) had risen at the rate of 7.6 per cent per year,
and M_2 (M_1, plus time deposits) had risen at a 9.7 per cent
annual rate.

From January, 1969, to July, 1969, these monetary growth

[2] Milton Friedman, "Have Monetary Policies Failed?," American Economic Association meeting, New Orleans, La., December 28, 1971.

rates were brought down to 5.1 and 3.5 per cent—"about the rates of growth that if long maintained would be consistent with steady noninflationary economic growth," said Dr. Friedman. "But, seeing no immediate results, the authorities then stepped too hard on the brake, bringing the growth rates down to 1.6 and 0.1 per cent from July, 1969, to February, 1970, thereby setting the stage for a sharper recession in 1970 than was necessary to restrain inflation."

After the recession began, the monetary authorities reversed their course, raising the money-supply growth rates to 5.5 per cent and 9.6 per cent from February, 1970, to January, 1971. Professor Friedman regarded those rates as "too high for the long run" but "at least understandable in light of the excessive earlier tightness." But there followed (in the wake of the November, 1970, election) a veritable "monetary explosion," with M_1 growing at an annual rate of over 12 per cent and M_2 over 15 per cent. This, said Dr. Friedman, was followed by another jamming on of the brakes through the rest of 1971, although he had "no doubt that we are in for another lurch to the opposite side of the road."

Given these changes in monetary policy, Professor Friedman said the changes in national income—expressed in current dollars—had been about what he and other monetarists expected. But, he admitted, he had not expected so much of the decline in "nominal" income to be in the output of real goods and services (and hence in employment) and so little in inflation. "The charge of failure," said Professor Friedman, "is that the rate of inflation was unusually slow to respond to the monetary changes and that an abnormal part of the change in nominal income was absorbed by the change in output—that the response was too late and too small. On this issue, I must confess that I made overly optimistic predictions in 1969 about how soon inflation could be expected to respond to the monetary slowdown. Inflation clearly did not react as rapidly as I predicted that it would."

"Chastened by this experience," said Friedman, he had re-examined the evidence for the postwar period and found that he had seriously underestimated in 1969 the typical time lag between the speeding up or the slowing down of the money supply and the subsequent speedup or slowdown in prices. He had been misled by the uncharacteristic mini-recession of 1967. He now found that money-supply changes hit industrial production pretty quickly—with about a three-month lag in the case of M_1 and a six-month lag in the case of M_2—but that money-supply changes affect consumer prices with a very much longer lag—averaging about twenty months later for M_1 and twenty-three months later for M_2. This lag before money changes affect prices, Friedman said, was "much larger than I expected." But politicians were impatient with the slowness of monetary policy to take effect.

"We have been driven into a widespread system of arbitrary and tyrannical control over our economic life," Friedman said, "not because 'economic laws are not working the way they used to' [a reference to his opponent, Chairman Arthur F. Burns, who so testified before the Joint Economic Committee on July 24, 1971 [3]], not because the classical

[3] Dr. Burns said that he found little or no progress against inflation. Although there had been some slowdown in the rate of rise in consumer prices in the earlier part of the year, he testified, there was evidence of a new acceleration in prices and wages by midyear. From January to July, 1971, consumer prices rose at an annual rate of 5.2 per cent and wholesale prices at an annual rate of 5.6 per cent. Burns said that an adjusted measure of wages rose a bit more in the first half of 1971 than in the previous two years: "This sustained sharp rise in wages during a period of substantial economic slack contrasts markedly with our experience in earlier recessions, when the rate of advance in wages typically dropped sharply or actually ceased." Even more fundamentally, from the standpoint of Administration monetarists, who contended that inflation was slowing down, the money supply was growing explosively in the first half of 1971.

medicine cannot, if properly applied, halt inflation, but because the public at large has been led to expect standards of performance that as economists we do not know how to achieve."

Perhaps, said Friedman, as knowledge advanced, economics could come closer to prescribing policies that would achieve higher standards of performance. Or perhaps, he worried, the "random perturbations inherent in the economic system" would make it impossible to achieve higher standards of price stability, high employment, and steady growth. Or perhaps, he said, even if there were policies that would attain such standards, considerations of what he called "political economy"—that is, politics—would make it impossible for these policies to be adopted.

"But whatever the future may hold in these respects," said Professor Friedman, "I believe that we economists in recent years have done vast harm—to society at large and to our profession in particular—by claiming more than we can deliver. We have thereby encouraged politicians to make extravagant promises, inculcate unrealistic expectations in the public at large, and promote discontent with reasonably satisfactory results because they fall short of the economists' promised land."

But there is another "perhaps" that Professor Friedman did not mention. Perhaps the highly industrialized, highly organized American economy no longer corresponds to the highly competitive and atomistic model of society on which classical economics and its policy prescriptions were based.

In the 1880's, when Senator John Sherman was campaigning for his Antitrust Act, he declared that "society is now disturbed by forces never felt before." If Congress refused to act to preserve competition, he warned, there would soon be "a trust for every production and a master to fix the price for every necessity of life." But the industrialist Andrew Carnegie was at the same time declaring that mass production involved heavy fixed charges, and that a chaotic market would wreck huge industries, cause capital to be wasted and depleted, and prevent national industrial development. The days of Adam Smith were "dead and gone," said Carnegie. James B. Dill (the lawyer who brought Carnegie and J. P. Morgan together to form the U.S. Steel Corporation) told Lincoln Steffens: "Trusts are natural, inevitable growths out of our social and economic conditions. You cannot stop them by force, with laws. They will sweep down like glaciers upon your police, courts, and States and wash them into flowing rivers. I am clearing the way for them."

As corporations grew in size and scope, there was a symbiosis between business and government. Not all liberals saw this as an undesirable trend. For instance, the founder of *The New Republic*, Herbert Croly, whose *Promise of American Life* had a major impact on Theodore Roosevelt, depicted the career of the great Republican political boss, Mark Hanna, as an effort to fuse business and government interests for the sake of the public welfare. "Of course," said Croly, "as a politician he could not help representing business because business was a part of himself—because business was in his eyes not simply money-making, but the most necessary kind of social labor." Hanna, said Croly, saw no evil in what he was trying to do; rather, he sought to keep alive "in his own policy and behavior the traditional association between business and politics, between private and public interest, which was gradually being shattered by the actual and irresistible development of American business and political life."

Was business's free-enterprise ideology, with its strong

antigovernment bias, its commitment to laissez faire, becoming outmoded? Was such an ideology damaging to the efficient operation of the economic system and the well-being of society in an age of industrialism? And was there need for a new balance—a new partnership—between government and business?

Half a century later, Lyndon B. Johnson answered that question with a resounding *yes.* At the end of 1964, President Johnson told the Business Council—the heads of America's largest corporations—that government and business must "operate in partnership," not as antagonists, to solve many problems, of which the foremost were accelerating the rate of economic expansion, maintaining price stability, strengthening the U.S. balance of payments, and "finding ways to reduce the tragically high rate of unemployment among teenagers, and assuring adequate economic opportunities for all our people not now in the mainstream of American prosperity." In attacking those problems, said Mr. Johnson, government and business have distinct and important roles to play: Government's responsibility was to produce a tax system that would not overburden businessmen or consumers and would maintain incentives for productive effort; to shape expenditure programs that would improve human and natural resources and make those social investments that are "needed to support private enterprise"; and to keep a "clear field" for private business in areas where competitive enterprise is the most efficient way of getting a job done. Government must develop fiscal and monetary policies that would promote balanced and stable growth and must be prepared to act "promptly and decisively when the nation is threatened by either recession or inflation." (Mr. Nixon could have made that same speech on August 15, 1971. In effect, he did make it thereafter—as at the White

House conference on the Industrial World Ahead on February 7, 1972.)

Business's responsibilities, said President Johnson, included producing "high-quality goods" and "new and improved" items, cutting production costs, and vigorously selling goods at home and abroad, while following employment policies that would offer workers both job security and incentives to increase their productivity and incomes. Business should build investment programs that would contribute to smooth expansion and avoid inventory problems that "have often been a source of economic instability in the past." (Government would help them do so, Mr. Nixon agreed—especially after reviving the investment tax credit and going the Johnson Administration one better with the accelerated depreciation system in 1971.)

But President Johnson's definition of business's responsibilities for advancing the public interest did not stop with such uncontroversial tasks. He included a plea to commercial banks not to raise interest rates (a theme to be repeated early and often by Mr. Johnson's protégé, John Connally, after he joined the Nixon Administration as Secretary of the Treasury). President Johnson said he was sure bankers realized that their own long-term interest was inseparable from the prosperity of the nation. (Check, Mr. Nixon.)

Mr. Johnson also emphasized a number of other ways that private business should serve its own and the public interest. It should respect the "noninflationary" wage-price guideposts first spelled out by President Kennedy's Council of Economic Advisers in 1962. (Check, Mr. Nixon, with variations, after August 15, 1971.)

Private business should put forth extra effort to increase its exports; the President later supplemented this plea for help in closing the foreign-payments gap with a strong call for "voluntary" programs to curb bank lending and direct investment abroad. (Check.) And Mr. Johnson called for private business to end discrimination against blacks in employment and to support increased educational and training programs for the poor. (Just a trifle less emphasis on this by Mr. Nixon.)

Implicit in all such Presidential recommendations and requests (Johnsonian or Nixonian) is the assumption that the free market does not provide satisfactory answers to many crucial economic and social problems facing the nation. To be sure, free-enterprisers would argue that government continuously undermines the free market and prevents it from doing its work of allocating resources efficiently and facilitating genuinely voluntary solutions to the nation's critical economic and social problems. But their critics— in economics, politics, and business—contend that in the American economic system as it now exists the market does not produce prompt and satisfactory answers to all economic and social problems, including inflation, unemployment, pollution, poverty, and urban decay.

But Mr. Nixon did not arrive in the White House with an economic philosophy so similar to Mr. Johnson's. On the contrary, Richard Nixon came to power in 1969 with a refurbished but essentially nostalgic free-enterprise creed that looked back well beyond the Johnson and Kennedy administrations—even beyond the Eisenhower Administration. In a sense, the 1968–69 Nixon creed, with heavy support from libertarians and conservatives, looked back to the days before the New Deal. At the beginning of his Administration in 1969, Mr. Nixon was prepared to make a serious effort to reverse the trend begun by Franklin D. Roosevelt in 1932 and to shrink the role of the federal government in the national economy.

When Dwight D. Eisenhower was elected President in 1952 and the Republicans finally took over the White House after two full decades of Democratic regimes, the conservatives in the party had hoped that Mr. Eisenhower would reverse the New Deal and Fair Deal policies, which they thought had been foisted upon the nation under the guise of the necessity of fighting depressions.

This was garbage, said their allies in the economics profession. As Professor Calvin B. Hoover of Duke University has noted, some leading economists—including Milton Friedman and George Stigler of the University of Chicago—declared that the American economy had undergone no fundamental change that warranted the economic policies of the New Deal and Fair Deal.[4] These economists thus challenged the entire basis of the "mixed economy" (or, as it was sometimes called, welfare capitalism, progressive capitalism, or the organizational economy), to distinguish it from old-style laissez-faire, individual-enterprise capitalism, in which government played a minimal role).

These conservative economists denied that collective bargaining by labor or government controls had been necessary to offset the "monopoly power" of big business since, they maintained, this monopoly power was largely a fiction. While this conclusion did not by any means represent a consensus among economists, the influence of the Chicago school of laissez-faire economics was extremely important on the conservative wing of the Republican Party. (Mr. Friedman's work on monetary theory and policy—which implied that there was a simple libertarian answer to cure the capitalist system of its worst weakness, its tendency for generating inflationary booms and busts that caused heavy

---

[4] Calvin B. Hoover, *The Economy, Liberty and the State* (New York: Twentieth Century Fund, 1959), pp. 252–53.

unemployment—constitutes a major brace for the traditional business ideology of keeping government's hands off the private economy.)

But President Eisenhower was not the candidate of the conservative wing of his party—he was an "Establishment" [5] President, although he made his peace with the conservatives. But in office he declined to undo the New Deal and Fair Deal economic changes in the American system. His Administration, in the words of Calvin Hoover, "signalized the permanence of the changed economic system."

As one example, consider the story of the Employment Act of 1946—which gave the federal government formal responsibility for promoting "maximum employment, production and purchasing power." The conservative wing of the Republican Party had tried to throw the Employment Act into disuse by failing to appropriate funds for the Council of Economic Advisers, which the act had created. Presi-

[5] It has been said that the American Establishment can be bounded by Arthur Goldberg on the left and Arthur Burns on the right. Both Democratic and Republican members of the Establishment offered the Presidential nomination to Dwight D. Eisenhower, before he decided to come out as a Republican in 1952. Richard H. Rovere, in a waggish essay in 1962, suggested that the "secret" chairman of the American Establishment was John J. McCloy, "Chairman of the Board of the Chase Manhattan Bank; once a partner in Cadawalader, de Gersdorff, Swaine & Wood, as well as, of course, Milbank, Tweed, Hope, Hadley & McCloy; former United States High Commissioner in Germany; former President of the World Bank; liberal Republican; chairman of the Ford Foundation and chairman . . . of the Council on Foreign Relations; Episcopalian." Religion apparently plays some role; in fact, although it has Jewish and Catholic members, E. Digby Baltzell calls it "the Protestant Establishment." However, William F. Buckley and the editors of the right-wing *National Review* see the Establishment as a kind of liberal conspiracy; and Senator Barry Goldwater, during the 1964 presidential campaign, suggested that it was an Eastern Establishment dominated by Wall Street tycoons. The Establishment has been somewhat pulled apart by the varying impacts of Vietnam, racial struggle, crime, and the tug of Richard Nixon as leader of the Republican Party. Today, it might be more appropriate to say that the Establishment is bounded on the left by John Kenneth Galbraith and on the right by Governor Nelson Rockefeller.

dent Eisenhower frustrated this effort. Indeed, he appointed Arthur Burns as Chairman of the Council, and Burns, despite his earlier anti-Keynesianism, behaved like a Keynesian in office.

But the dreams of the conservatives in the Republican Party, and of their economic advisers, did not die. They did not accept Professor Hoover's verdict that the Eisenhower Administration marked the passing of the old order and the consolidation of the new. With the candidacy of Senator Barry Goldwater for the Presidency in 1964, their hopes soared. Here was a man who really represented change in a libertarian direction—and Milton Friedman became his chief economic adviser. The libertarian hopes even survived the Goldwater electoral landslide.

And then came Richard Nixon in 1968—and at last the libertarians and the conservatives were in, with a real chance to create what Mr. Nixon himself grandiloquently called "the Second American Revolution."

The effort to turn back the clock lasted two and a half years. Is it now really over? Did August 15 finally and irrevocably shatter the dream of the libertarians? (One of them pronounced grimly, "American fascism arrived on August 15, 1971.") Did the failure of monetarism and laissez faire on wages and prices—as judged by Mr. Nixon and the politicos, whatever the economists may say—truly signalize the permanence of the "mixed economy," far more conclusively than the Eisenhower Administration had done?

The answer is probably yes—considering both the structure of the American economy and the nature of American politics. Professor Friedman and the monetarists contend that inflation is strictly a monetary phenomenon and can be ended by a rule for monetary growth. But inflation can also be regarded as a struggle that goes on among social groups —in which the government itself can be regarded as one of the social groups. Workers push for higher wages than productivity advances will justify; employers try to increase their profits and their command of real resources for expanding their capacity to produce; consumers struggle to get more goods—or at least to keep other groups from grabbing their share; government—or the politicians who run the government—may want to expand their share of resources to meet foreign-policy objectives, to meet domestic needs, or to win support from particular groups in the electorate. Especially if unemployment threatens, government hesitates to cut back either private demand or its own share.

In these circumstances, the monetary authorities face a nasty dilemma: Shall they accede to the desires of the competing groups and provide the reserves that let the inflationary game go on? Or shall they say no, and assume responsibility for the slump that may follow?

If the monetary authorities are not to be forced into this position—a position that they cannot politically endure, because a sitting government that hopes for re-election will not permit it—what can be done? The trade-off between inflation and unemployment can be improved. As the Kennedy and Johnson administrations had done before it, this, in a nutshell, is what the Nixon Administration sought to do when it launched the New Economic Policy. It is trying to suppress inflation by price, wage, dividend, and rent controls, while it boosts total spending through tax cuts and higher government outlays to reduce unemployment.

How permanent is the change?

George Shultz, the director of the Office of Management and Budget and, with Herbert Stein, one of the two strongest enemies of wage-price controls before the freeze, has since decided that the recent historical context has been just right for controls. For controls to work, said Mr. Shultz, three conditions must be satisfied: "The deck needs to be stacked in your favor"—that is, inflation already should be slowing down—monetary and fiscal policy should be set to generate neither too much nor too little demand; and the economy should be rising but there should still be enough slack to permit strong productivity gains. Under such conditions, he implied, controls can make everything just a bit better and accelerate the recovery while preserving reasonable price stability.

What about the converse of Mr. Shultz's thesis? Should controls be dropped when one or more of his conditions are no longer present—when inflation is no longer slowing down, when the money supply has been growing too fast or the budget deficit is too big, or when there is no longer enough slack in the economy? Early in 1972 there were strong hints not only from Mr. Shultz and Mr. Stein but from President Nixon that the Administration would end controls as soon as possible. Mr. Nixon pointedly—and publicly—disagreed with Paul McCracken, who, on leaving Washington, had said that some form of wage-price restraints might be needed for years to come.

Decontrol would appease the hostility to Mr. Nixon of right-wingers within his own party; these conservatives might have nowhere else to go, but Mr. Nixon would still not want a disgruntled right wing on his hands. Further, the unpopularity of wage-price controls seems likely to grow as time wears on—especially if inequities in their administration increase.

But premature talk of decontrol was not making the task of the price controllers any easier early in 1972. The head of the Price Commission, C. Jackson Grayson, Jr., an outspoken and determined man, warned that such talk from the White House would be "damaging" to the stabilization program.

Again, in one of its characteristic shifts of position, the Nixon Administration firmed up its support of controls. There was still anxiety at the White House about decontrolling prematurely; Mr. Nixon would pay a heavy penalty for making a mistake too far ahead of the election. In the Economic Report of the President, Herbert Stein said that the sentence of which he was proudest read: "Speculation that the Administration will abandon the controls prematurely—out of fatigue, ideological aversion, or other causes—is groundless." The report went on to say that the Administration, having embarked on that course, "has no intention of departing from it in circumstances where it would risk either resumption of inflation or the need to reimpose the controls."

More fundamentally, however, there remains the long-term issue: what national economic policy should be for reconciling price stability with full employment. Can this be done simply by finding the politically acceptable point on the "Phillips curve"—the O.K. rate of inflation that goes with the O.K. rate of unemployment? But no such politically acceptable point may exist. A number of leading economists have come to regard the Phillips curve as the last gasp of an unadulterated Keynesian policy. They feel that for years to come—perhaps permanently—fiscal and monetary policy will have to be supplemented by wage-price restraints, manpower policies, and direct job-creating policies—such as more public service jobs—both for improving the trade-off between unemployment and inflation and for the sake of dealing with urgent social problems. But all this is not acceptable Nixonian doctrine.

Despite Mr. Nixon's switch to the New Economic Policy, it was by no means clear that he had really accepted the evolution of economic policies extending from Franklin D. Roosevelt to Lyndon B. Johnson. Richard Nixon has a somewhat different constituency from theirs—not only the major part of the business community but a broad slice of suburbia and Middle America—and he has demonstrated a remarkable ability to go to his left or his right (and to run reverses). He can commit himself to a policy or a principle with tremendous rhetorical flourish and drop it at a moment's notice. He is in no sense an economist; he is, through and through, a party man.

Joseph A. Schumpeter, the Austrian economist who became the outstanding philosopher and interpreter of American capitalism, wrote:

A party is not, as classical doctrine (or Edmund Burke) would have us believe, a group of men who intend to promote public welfare "upon some principle on which they are all agreed." This rationalization is so dangerous because it is so tempting. For all parties will of course, at any given time, provide themselves with a stock of principles or planks, and these principles or planks may be as characteristic of the party that adopts them and as important for its success as the brands of goods a department store sells are characteristic of it and important for its success. But the department store cannot be defined in terms of its brands and a party cannot be defined in terms of its principles. A party is a group whose members propose to act in concert in the competitive struggle for political power. If that were not so it would be impossible for different parties to adopt exactly or almost exactly the same program. Yet this happens as everyone knows. Party and machine politicians are simply the response to the fact that the electoral mass is incapable of action other than a stampede, and they constitute an attempt to regulate political competition exactly similar to the corresponding practices of a trade association. The psychotechnics of party management and party advertising, slogans and marching tunes, are not accessories. They are of the essence of politics. So is the political boss.

Nixonomics is of the essence of politics, and the psychotechnics of party management and advertising explain its extraordinary range, diversity, flexibility, and style. It comprehends Friedmanism and Keynesianism, laissez faire and price controls, mercantilism and free trade, the ideologies of free enterprise and social responsibilities. It might be described as the most comprehensive economics in the history of the world.

19. The Rhythm
of Nixonomics

The aim of President Nixon's original wage-price-rent freeze and somewhat more flexible Phase Two controls was to ensure that infusions of money, resulting from tax cuts and higher government spending, would go into creating more goods and jobs—not just feed inflation.

That combined dose of controls and fiscal stimulus worked reasonably well in 1972. The rate of growth in real output of the national economy accelerated; unemployment shrank, and the rate of wage and price increase slowed down. But the results in the international sector were disappointing; the President's Council of Economic Advisers, in the 1973 Economic Report, euphemized, "Some progress was made on the international front, but it was greatly overshadowed by developments in the domestic economy." In cold numbers, the United States ran a foreign-trade deficit of nearly $7 billion in 1972, the worst in its history, following the $2.7 billion deficit of 1971, the first of this century.

"Nonetheless," said the CEA's economic report, "by the end of 1972 there was a strong sense of optimism about the progress that had been achieved and the ability to find answers to some of the problems that remained."

In that rosy atmosphere—to which the President's landslide electoral victory over Senator George McGovern had contributed—Mr. Nixon and his economic advisers decided that the time had come to start dismantling wage-price controls and moving back toward a free economy. In the flush of victory, Mr. Nixon was apparently eager to rehabilitate his conservative ideology.

He was encouraged to do so by his top economic advisers. George P. Shultz, the University of Chicago economist who had come to Washington as Mr. Nixon's Secretary of Labor, and who had served as the first directcor of the newly reorganized Office of Management and Budget, had now become Secretary of the Treasury, and, even more importantly, the designated chief economic adviser to the President.

Less than a month after the November, 1972, election, the President and his economic aides decided to shift from Phase Two controls to looser "voluntary" Phase Three wage-price restraints. The logic behind the shift was embodied in what history may remember as Shultz's Law: that price and wage controls work best when they are needed least. In a meeting with newspapermen in Washington on January 8, 1973, Mr. Shultz said that he felt the Administration had got "some mileage" out of controls, especially in combination with the simultaneous tax cuts and new inter-national monetary arrangements that made up the President's New Economic Policy. "If we were going to impose controls," he said, "our timing could not have been better," because of the slack in the economy and the opportunity to break inflationary expectations and pressures of labor and other groups. For the year ahead, however, Mr. Shultz said he was concerned about putting too much reliance on direct controls, because the slack was disappearing. The focus of the anti-inflation effort, he said, would now shift from controls to over-all budget and fiscal policy.

There was obviously some anxiety within the Administration about lifting controls prematurely, especially as evidence began to accumulate in December and early January about the acceleration of inflation—especially the skyrocketing of food prices. But, once a major government decision has been made, it gathers momentum day by day, and may become almost unstoppable.

The President's Council of Economic Advisers, in its January report, spelled out the official rationalization for loosening controls: "A case could . . . be made for continuing the anti-inflationary influence of controls in 1973. But the experience of 1972 also suggested a number of dangers to be avoided. Although the cost of controls in retarding and distorting economic activity had apparently thus far not been great, these costs seemed to be rising. They could be much more significant in 1973 as the program aged and as the economy came closer to its potential. The number of instances of excess demand would multiply, and the relative price ceilings established by the system would become more potent sources of distortions. More and more companies would hit their profit-margin ceilings, with adverse consequences for cost control and for investment incentives."

So, with its Phase Three wage-price restraints and so-called statutory jawboning, the Nixon Administration took a big step back toward where it began in 1969, but it did not go all the way. It kept three particularly inflation-prone industries—food, health, and construction—under mandatory wage and price standards. But there had been no price controls on agricultural products at the farm level, and there would be none under Phase Three. Food prices, which had been rising steadily for months, took off like a second-stage rocket in December, 1972, zooming up by 5.2 per cent, or more than 60 per cent at an annual rate. That event created a poor psychological climate for the decontrol program.

Mr. Nixon was trying to throw much bigger supplies of meat, milk, cotton, feed grains, and other farm products into the balance, hoping to outweigh rapidly rising demand. He was doing this both by dropping or cutting import quotas and by increasing acreage allotments. However, he had by no means abandoned his determination to keep farm income up and rising. He intended to work the magic trick of pushing farm income up and prices down by calling idle acreage into production while only "adjusting"—not eliminating—payments to farmers.

George Shultz called the three sectors remaining under mandatory controls—food, health, and construction—"un-Galbraithian" industries. All are made up of many small economic units, rather than being huge corporate or labor collectivities. But what all three industries also have in common (and this may not be all that "un-Galbraithian") is a heavy dependency upon the federal government. The government has an arsenal of weapons, ranging from import quotas to medical payments to construction contracts, that it could deploy in all three sectors.

In the much vaster reaches of the economy, however, Mr. Shultz was ready to gamble on an essentially voluntary program in which business and labor would determine for themselves whether their pay or wage conduct conforms to guidelines.

The soft-spoken Treasury Secretary claimed that he was not simply going back to Kennedy-Johnson Administration–type guidelines, because the Nixon Administration would retain legal power to enforce them. It was keeping what Mr. Shultz called "a stick in the closet"—authority to assert jurisdiction over cases where pay or price actions violate the guidelines.

The great question worrying business and labor, however, was when and whether and how severely the Administration would use the stick in the closet. Was it a club, a whiffle-ball bat, or a twig?

Skeptics feared that the Nixon Administration would lack what one of them called the "good judgment, finesse, vigor, and guts" to fight any violations down. They said that the Administration's essential move was to relax profit-margin controls in order to stimulate investment—but that Wall Street celebration would not last long, if greater freedom for profits to rise under the new formulas were matched by greater freedom for wages to rise. In fact, Wall Street soon went into a slump in reaction to Phase Three. Curiously enough, the business and financial community was far from pleased by Mr. Nixon's lurch to the right.

Mr. Nixon's budget and fiscal policy for his second term marked even more dramatically his countermarch to the right. In his second inaugural address and his budget, economic, and State of the Union messages, the President hammered home his dominant theme: Social programs must now be cut back—and military programs expanded—now that the Vietnam war was over.

To be sure, Mr. Nixon did not use that kind of simple language to describe what he was proposing to do. He declared that he was going to "chart a new course for America." But to liberals it looked as though he was trying to reverse the course of public policy that the nation had pursued for forty years and turn back toward the traditional Republican philosophy of Presidents Harding, Coolidge, and Hoover—before the Great Depression shook the nation's faith in unrestricted free enterprise and before Franklin D. Roosevelt's New Deal greatly expanded the social role of government.

Yet it would misrepresent Mr. Nixon's economic philosophy to suggest that he merely wanted to return to economic laissez faire; on the contrary, he had proved himself a Keynesian, more than willing to run large budgetary deficits when needed to restore the economy to high employment. And, as his wage-price freeze and subsequent controls had demonstrated, he was willing—when necessary to restore price stability—to have government intervene directly in the holy of holies of the capitalist system, the price- and wage-setting process. Paradoxically, it was in fact the relative success of Mr. Nixon's Keynesian fiscal and monetary policy, and of his Galbraithian wage-price policy, that had emboldened him at the start of his second term drastically to reduce the social role of the federal government. In gaining a reasonable degree of control over both inflation and unemployment, the President considered that he could essentially trust individual and business decisions in the marketplace to determine how the nation's welfare could best be advanced.

In an appeal to the nation, just before he sent his fiscal 1974 budget to Congress, Mr. Nixon told his radio audience: "What is at stake is your job, your taxes, the prices you pay and whether the money you earn by your work is spent by you for what you want, or by government for what someone else wants."

There were three basic issues wrapped up in that sentence: the impact of the budget on employment and inflation; the level of taxes and the distribution of tax burdens; and the appropriate allocation of national resources.

On the first issue of fiscal impact, the President's budget in calling for a ceiling of $269 billion in fiscal 1974 had sought to implement the broad economic strategy of shifting from fairly tight controls and a stimulative budget to loose controls and a moderately restrictive budget. Conservatives could well argue that, in view of residual inflationary pressures and the booming economy, the budget should have been more restrictive; liberals, dubious about the likelihood of regaining 4 per cent unemployment, could argue the opposite. On balance, however, the President's middle course—given the expectation of a $115-billion increase in gross national product during calendar 1973—seemed a reasonable compromise.

But, on the second major issue of tax policy, would Congress accept the President's dictum that under no circumstances should taxes be raised? Mr. Nixon's spokesmen had made it clear that any new expenditure programs not already in his budget would have to be substituted for another in what the President had implied was an already skin-tight budget. This rule would even apply to future programs for helping to rebuild war-devastated Vietnam—for which there was no provision in the budget, though it appeared to be required by the cease-fire agreement.

Mr. Nixon's no-tax-increase principle was in any case misleading; the highly regressive Social Security taxes—taxes that hit the poor harder than the rich—would be rapidly rising to cover outlays on social insurance, which totaled $61.7 billion in fiscal 1972 and would reach $87.6 billion in fiscal 1975.

What the President's no-tax-increase line really meant was freezing the increasingly regressive tax system. Mr. Nixon's spokesmen said that the President might still submit a program of tax reform, but it was clear from their earlier statements that they expected only slight increases, if any, in the revenues that would be yielded by the kind of tax reform they had in mind.

The third budgetary issue involved the programs that the President was proposing to cut or increase, his national priorities. Unquestionably Mr. Nixon and his aides had proposed many necessary and long overdue cuts, including some direct payments to farmers, export subsidies, aid to so-called impacted schools near federal facilities, extra highways, and so forth. But other cuts—and missing programs—appeared to be a retreat from efforts to deal with the nation's unsolved health, education, welfare, and other social problems. For Mr. Nixon had at best half a program—he had done much cutting but little or no constructive replacement. Most conspicuously, there was no welfare reform in his new budget; his celebrated Family Assistance Program had vanished.

While the President had been ruthless on social programs, he had been tender with the defense budget. What he called, with the Vietnam war over, "a true peacetime budget in every sense of the word," called for defense outlays to rise from $76.4 billion in fiscal 1973 to $81.1 billion in fiscal 1974, and to $85.5 billion in fiscal 1975.

This military budget increase was described by the White House as virtually all due to "pay and price" increases—and, to be sure, these did play a big part, as inflation continued and the nation converted to a volunteer army. But the military expenses were also due to many ongoing programs, such as the B-1 manned bomber, the Trident submarine, the Safeguard missile site, new nuclear carriers, plans for national air defense, over-all military force levels. Similarly, Mr. Nixon proposed no cuts in the half-billion dollars going to maritime subsidies; on the contrary, maritime subsidies would go on rising.

As the head of an Administration that had been anything but immune from the influence of special interests such as milk, textile, oil, steel, aircraft, maritime, and assorted defense producers, Mr. Nixon certainly knew what he was talking about when he urged the people at the start of 1973 to make their views known to the Congress, because "they hear from the special interests; let them hear from you."

Thus does Mr. Nixon proceed from opportunism to ideology and back to opportunism, as the situation requires. Crises—in prices, jobs, or the international monetary front —scatter his ideology to the winds. But, with the return of stability, the conservative ideology comes back like a homing pigeon. The cycle that leads from ideology to crisis, from crisis to opportunism, from opportunism to stability, and from stability back to ideology is the basic pattern of Nixonomics—and the underlying rhythm of Mr. Nixon's Presidency.

In the second week of February, 1973, what at first seemed like a minor flurry over the weakness of the Italian lira and the transfer of funds by speculators into Swiss francs blew up into a full-fledged monetary crisis, and waves of selling buffeted the United States dollar. In the space of a few days, more than 6 billion American dollars were sold for German marks, Japanese yen, and other foreign currencies. In Germany alone, speculators unloaded $4 billion in two days. The immediate effect was a lowering of the dollar in relation to foreign currencies; the danger was a collapse of the world monetary system.

As redefined by the Smithsonian Agreement of December, 1971, the monetary system called for fixed rates for major currencies within a narrow range. To maintain the rates, central banks were committed to buying or selling currencies to balance the demand-supply situation whenever pressures built up. If the demand-supply ratio became excessive, however—as had become the case in the soaring demand for marks and yen in exchange for dollars—the fixed rates had to be changed or the system would break down. Such a breakdown was threatened in early February because the Germans and Japanese—whose currencies were the strongest in the system—were resisting an upward adjustment of their currencies that would make their export goods less competitive with American or other products.

President Nixon, British Prime Minister Heath, West German Chancellor Willy Brandt, and French President Georges Pompidou hastily conferred by telephone in what was taken as an effort to keep the monetary crisis from ripping apart the fabric of Western economic and political relations. The finance ministers of the major European states met in Paris for urgent consultations to prevent the monetary upheaval from wrecking the Common Market. And the American Under Secretary of the Treasury for Monetary

Affairs, Paul A. Volcker, took off in an Air Force plane for Tokyo and then over the North Pole to Europe, to work out a deal with the other major financial powers.

The dollar had been staggered by a combination of blows:

• The news that the United States in 1972 suffered the worst trade deficit in its history—close to $7 billion. The resulting excess supply of dollars to Europe tended to drive the price of the dollar down—just as any commodity, milk, for example, in excess on the market will be driven down in price.

• Fears that the Smithsonian Agreement, hailed by Mr. Nixon as "the most significant monetary achievement in the history of the world," had failed. By that agreement, the dollar was devalued and other currencies upvalued in various amounts, yielding a net dollar devaluation of 11 to 12 per cent. That devaluation was supposed to make American goods cheaper and foreign goods dearer, and thus curb the outflow of dollars. In early February, the markets abandoned that hope.

• The concern by investors around the world that American inflation was still not under control. What triggered inflationary expectations was the announcement by Treasury Secretary Shultz that Phase Two price and wage controls were being replaced by the flexible, voluntary restraints of Phase Three. That announcement had coincided with the news of rapidly rising food and other wholesale prices. Later statements of President Nixon, Secretary Shultz, and other Administration spokesmen that the program was really tough—with the "stick in the closet" ready for use in bashing price or wage raisers into submission—had not remedied the initial impression that Phase Three was an untimely step toward Phase Zero.

And so the dollar was devalued again—this time by 10 per cent. This second devaluation by Mr. Nixon was necessitated by the chaos in the international money markets and persistent weakness in the American trade and payments position, but it scarcely provided occasion for him to claim a triumph for the way he had managed the American economy, as he sought to do. On the contrary, the Administration's policies had done much to exacerbate a situation that had been in the making for a decade—partly because of the Vietnam war.

It was not as if monetary crises, like hurricanes, were acts of God. The Administration had contributed to the weakening of the dollar by scuttling wage and price controls in a deal to obtain organized labor's political support—at a time when the economy was starting to boom, when food prices were skyrocketing, and when new figures on the worsening trade deficit were alarming world financial markets.

Mr. Nixon's fiscal and monetary policies since the election had been no more reassuring than his scuttling of wage and price controls. Having seriously eroded the United States tax base, particularly by chopping taxes on business, Mr. Nixon emerged from the election with a new sacred principle: He would never raise taxes; the guilt for any tax increases would be on Congress's head, not his. After piling up deficits totaling almost $80 billion in his first term—with more deficits ahead, despite the rapidly climbing economy—Mr. Nixon was still unwilling to consider raising taxes. Instead, he meant to cut social programs that might improve the trade-off between inflation and unemployment.

In the area of monetary policy, the Administration had put Arthur Burns, chairman of its Committee on Interest and Dividends, in the feckless position of trying to jawbone down the interest rates that, as chairman of the Federal Reserve Board, his highly stimulative monetary actions had caused to rise.

It seemed highly unlikely that a strong dollar could be restored until the Administration convincingly demonstrated that it was willing to use whatever tools were required to achieve both stable prices and full employment and that it had not simply reverted, for political or ideological reasons, to the discredited economic doctrine with which Mr. Nixon began his Presidency.

"In my end is my beginning."—T. S. Eliot

Index